Guy de Maupassant

Titles in the series Critical Lives present the work of leading cultural figures of the modern period. Each book explores the life of the artist, writer, philosopher or architect in question and relates it to their major works.

In the same series

Guy de Maupassant

Christopher Lloyd

REAKTION BOOKS

Published by Reaktion Books Ltd
Unit 32, Waterside
44–48 Wharf Road
London N1 7UX, UK

www.reaktionbooks.co.uk

First published 2020
Copyright © Christopher Lloyd 2020

Printed and bound in India by Replika Press Pvt. Ltd

A catalogue record for this book is available from the British Library

ISBN 978 1 78914 197 9

Contents

1

A Life

Guy de Maupassant (1850–1893) was and remains the most celebrated French storyteller of the nineteenth century, both in France and internationally. The enduring appeal of his stories derives from not only understated artistry and craftsmanship (the ability to entice and engage readers by creating drama, pathos and irony in a few succinct pages written with limpid precision and sensual clarity) but the universality of his characters and their aspirations and misfortunes. The people who inhabit Maupassant's three hundred stories are drawn from a wide range of social classes and races – from peasants to politicians and intellectuals; from society ladies and prostitutes to nuns and priests; from servants, soldiers and sailors to aristocrats and landowners; from Europeans of many nationalities to Africans; not to mention criminals, lunatics, animals and imaginary beings. While these characters offer us a fascinating historical panorama of late nineteenth-century France, an exotic glimpse of a bygone social world, their daily preoccupations and conflicts remain instantly recognizable: achieving personal fulfilment and social integration, enduring the grim consequences of warfare, poverty and disease, broken families and unhappy marriages, or the stigma and trauma of unwanted pregnancy, illegitimacy and other forms of abuse.

However, Maupassant was much more than a beguiling storyteller or the pessimistic and disabused fictional chronicler of Third Republic France. His career as a professional writer lasted only twelve years before it was brutally cut short by the horrendous consequences of untreatable syphilis: chronic sickness, a failed suicide attempt, insanity, paralysis and death after confinement for eighteen months in a clinic. His ultimate mental and physical degradation and disintegration inevitably invite comparisons with the obsessive recurrence of such themes throughout his writing. Yet his most striking and attractive characteristic is actually his prodigious energy and vitality, both as a man and an author. Between 1880 and 1890 he never stopped writing, producing hundreds of stories and essays for newspapers and reviews, in addition to publishing fifteen volumes of stories reassembled in six full-length novels, three books of travel writing, a volume of verse and several plays. His athletic prowess also aroused admiration and envy, enabling him to cover vast distances as a rower and walker and enjoy sexual relations with a large number of women from a wide range of social classes and stations. Contrary to the rather dour, reclusive figure depicted by some spiteful colleagues and ingenuous biographers, Maupassant was good at making friends who liked and assisted him in his rapid progress from obscure government clerk to wealthy, internationally renowned writer. In fact, Maupassant's network of friends and acquaintances covered an astonishing range, from members of social elites such as government ministers, titled aristocrats, famous artists and writers, to wealthy lawyers and businessmen and quite ordinary people like the sailors who crewed his yacht and his personal valet and early biographer François Tassart. And although he rejected the conventional ties of marriage (having neither wife nor children), he devoted a great deal of time and money to supporting his own distressing and demanding family and other dependants (such as his wastrel brother, neurotic mother and ineffectual father).

For all his ironic detachment, Maupassant's private and public life is inseparable from this very substantial body of literary work (to which should be added the hundreds of letters in his extant correspondence). He continues to entertain, engage and enlighten twenty-first-century readers throughout the world, whereas many of his late nineteenth-century contemporaries are nowadays read only by French literary specialists (indeed, Maupassant's posthumous sales and readership are far greater than the audience he reached during his lifetime). His phenomenal trajectory has always fascinated commentators, whose admiration may be tempered by envy of his success or pity at his tragic decline. Since the 1890s, Maupassant has attracted a large number of critics and biographers, including some excellent studies in English published in the mid-twentieth century in the USA and UK. However, although French publishers continue to produce very lengthy biographies – and specialized academic studies on specific themes and works appear regularly in many languages – for a long time no British or American publisher has brought out an updated critical biography in English aimed at a broad readership.[1] Reaktion's Critical Lives series, with its relatively compact format, demands a somewhat more selective and accessible approach, in effect an extended biographical essay concentrating on the most significant aspects of Maupassant's life and career during the brilliant decade before his decline and demise. This introductory chapter therefore offers a critical, contextualizing overview of Maupassant's life, thought and reputation, while six subsequent chapters focus on the important stages and achievements in the evolution of his creative life and legacy. Titles throughout are cited in French, with English translations when the work in question is discussed in detail, and given that Maupassant's main claim to fame is as a writer of stories and novels, two chapters focus specifically on his shorter and longer fiction.

The aims of this book are primarily to explore and analyse this interaction between life and work in all its diversity, to situate Maupassant in the literary and social context of nineteenth-century France, to discuss the initial production and reception of his writing, and how its reception and reproduction (in different editions and media) have evolved in the twentieth and twenty-first centuries. For example, most readers invariably first encounter Maupassant's work in posthumous anthologies of stories (whether in French or translation) selected by editors who at best can offer only a partial impression of his work and who at worst unscrupulously truncate, expurgate, mistranslate or plagiarize the writer for their own benefit.[2] It is important to counteract such distortions by offering a more impartial account of his life and achievements as a writer from a broader, historical perspective, while at the same time conveying the texture and sensuousness of his writing, the sound and modalities of his authorial voice, in representative key works. Biographers invariably stress Maupassant's personal suffering and bleak pessimism; thus Georges Normandy asserts that his grim destiny recalls Greek tragedy.[3] Maupassant's public and private writings certainly offer innumerable gloomy examples of his own pessimism – such as his notorious trenchant statement, 'I have desired everything but enjoyed nothing', in his autobiographical travelogue *Sur l'eau* (1888) – and that he wrote only to earn money, as claimed in an 1884 letter to Marie Bashkirtseff. But there are also many counter-examples, which express erotic delight and pantheistic rapture; thus he writes to Gisèle d'Estoc in January 1881, 'I love the flesh of women, in the same way I love the grass, the rivers, the sea,' presenting his writing as celebrating a sensual absorption in the beauty of nature.[4] Understanding Maupassant involves accounting for, rather than ignoring, such apparently contradictory postures towards the joys and miseries of existence and artistic creation.

Henri René Albert Guy de Maupassant was born on 5 August 1850 at the Château de Miromesnil in Normandy. His parents, Gustave and Laure (both born in 1821), belonged to the wealthy provincial bourgeoisie. Gustave had re-established the family's legal entitlement to the pseudo-aristocratic *particule* 'de' in 1846

Maupassant's grandiose birthplace, the Château de Miromesnil.

(their ancestors had discreetly dropped it after the 1789 revolution).
Although he (that is, Maupassant) affected to disdain titles,
honours and decorations and those who sought or displayed them,
Guy de Maupassant undoubtedly thought that he personally
belonged to the dominant social elite by virtue of literary genius
if not birth, and was fascinated by the intricacies and hazards of
social status and promotion. His younger brother Hervé was born
in May 1856. From 1859, the family's prosperous, leisurely existence
was disrupted by financial problems, which forced Gustave to
seek employment at a bank and subsequently at a stockbroker's
in Paris; a year later, Laure returned to Étretat in Normandy with
the two children and ceased to live with her husband (they were
legally separated in 1863, since full divorce was impossible). Given
the many depictions of unhappy families riven by infidelity and
discord in Maupassant's writings, biographers often present this
parental separation as deeply troubling and significant to the young
Maupassant's later works (citing for example the story 'Garçon, un
bock!', which shows a life ruined by such primal trauma). In fact,

we know very little about the author's childhood (and fictional characters rarely reflect his personality and feelings so overtly). Both brothers seem to have lived happily with their mother (whose comfortable income derived from her own land and property), and all three remained on cordial (albeit distant) terms with Gustave. Laure was an affectionate but demanding mother, who suffered from depression and hypochondria in her self-imposed solitude, whereas her husband was an easy-going man about town and amateur painter whose affairs rarely prospered. Indeed by 1882 further misjudged investments had increased his financial losses to 80,000 francs (the equivalent of about £1,000,000 today);[5] from

Maupassant aged seven.

this point onwards, Maupassant's parents and brother would become increasingly dependent on the industrious writer to subsidize them.

In 1863 Guy was sent to a Catholic boarding school in Yvetot, where he was at first a docile and moderately ambitious pupil. A letter to his mother (who was highly cultivated and probably the woman to whom he remained closest throughout his life) from May 1864 shows him earnestly competing for prizes in Latin (the only foreign language which he knew in any depth) but aspiring to acquire a rowing boat. Four years later, however, he was expelled from this ecclesiastic institution for writing impious verse in which he lamented 'dans le cloître solitaire / Où nous sommes ensevelis, / Nous ne connaissons sur la terre / Que soutanes et que surplis . . .' ('In this solitary cloister / To which we are bound, / We know only priests and friars / In our earthly round': *Des vers*, 1880).[6] He took further revenge in an unsympathetic article about secondary schools written in 1885, describing them as 'those establishments for moral torture and physical brutalization', which inhibit the full development of the young with their rigid discipline and outmoded curriculum.[7] Following this minor rebellion, Maupassant was transferred to the *lycée* in Rouen, where he passed the *baccalauréat ès lettres* in 1869 before enrolling as a law student in Paris.

Whereas such educational achievements have become an unremarkable norm for most young people in twenty-first-century France, in the pyramidal social hierarchy of the nineteenth century they remained the prerogative of a privileged minority. Although by the 1870s most children attended primary school, less than 3 per cent of an age group continued to fee-paying secondary education; only 2 per cent of the male population gained the then prestigious *bac*, and there were fewer than 10,000 university students in 1870, nearly all of them drawn from the upper and middle bourgeoisie, which numbered less than 1 million people (from a total population of 36 million). Secondary schooling was neither egalitarian nor vocational, but intended to transmit the hierarchical values of the social elite to younger generations. Without such qualifications, entry into elite professions was virtually impossible, especially for children from subordinate social groups, although they were no guarantee of advancement.[8]

Military service remained an obligation for all young men in Second Empire France, though conscription was determined by a lottery and the wealthy could pay a volunteer to replace them. However, the outbreak of war with Germany in July 1870 meant that Maupassant was immediately called up; as an educated man he was sent to the supply corps in Rouen rather than a combat regiment. Nevertheless, this unnecessary war was the most disruptive event in his early life, giving him direct experience of death and destruction on a scale he would otherwise never have witnessed (he narrowly escaped being taken prisoner while delivering orders to the front line). For the authoritarian regime of Napoleon III and the nation, it was a humiliating catastrophe: within six months, the empire had been overthrown, the French armies routed and an armistice signed, the outcome of which was the loss of two provinces to Germany and a revolutionary insurrection in Paris in spring 1871, repressed with extreme brutality by the new French government. Maupassant's scorn for self-serving and incompetent political and military leaders undoubtedly derived from this debacle (as did his awareness of the suffering, courage and occasional heroism of those in humbler positions).

Gustave was finally able to buy his son out of the army in November 1871, but his relative impoverishment meant he could offer Guy only a modest annual allowance of 600 francs. Like his father, Maupassant was therefore obliged to seek paid employment and for the next eight years became a clerk in two government ministries, a period of bureaucratic drudgery which he presents as soul-destroying and loathsome (although his contemporary and friend the novelist J.-K. Huysmans had no difficulty in combining his literary career with 32 years of dutiful service in the Ministry of the Interior). Even the unrewarding jobs which Maupassant eventually obtained required obsequious supplications supported by influential figures. When he was appointed to the Ministry of the Navy and Colonies in 1872, it was initially as an unpaid supernumerary (rather like the interns of today's graduate job market), with a permanent position and annual salary of 1,500 francs from February 1873.

Maupassant's letters from this period reveal a constant anxiety and resentment about lacking money (and the services and pleasures it bought), including detailed accounts of his meagre monthly budgets. Despite his complaints of poverty and his father's stinginess, his salary was about the average wage of a male junior clerk or unskilled manual labourer. Ordinary people in the late nineteenth century still lived precarious lives, with impoverishment or even destitution a constant threat, as indeed so many of Maupassant's stories reveal. His pride in his exceptional success and promotion to the ranks of the wealthy perhaps reinforced his awareness of and sympathy for those trapped in petty misery and their struggles to escape it. By late 1878 his salary had risen significantly to 2,000 francs, but his dissatisfaction with his working conditions and hostile superiors drove him to seek a transfer to the Ministry of Public Instruction, finally achieved after tortuous negotiations in February 1879. Maupassant actually says little about his work, other than that it is dull and time-consuming; the ministry, with its desiccated bureaucrats, petty tyrants and wearisome routines and rituals is endured as a sort of purgatory, although it also provided the writer with excellent material for his many well-observed stories about the servitude and occasional grandeur of a large sector of the French population (there were 700,000 minor officials in 1870). After June 1880 Maupassant took extended periods of sick leave from which he never returned to government service: he had at last become an independent writer able to live well off sales of his articles, stories and books.

How Maupassant launched and managed his career as a journalist and creative writer (of poems, plays and fiction) will be discussed in detail in the following chapters. At this stage, it is worth noting that achieving publication and recognition required not merely unusual personal talent and exceptional energy but the ability to attract sponsors and mentors able and willing to exert influence in his favour: sympathetic editors and publishers, as well as established authors, the most celebrated of whom was Gustave Flaubert, a long-standing family friend. Maupassant's breakthrough occurred only in 1880, when he was nearly thirty years old, after struggling to combine office work and sporting pastimes with writing and negotiating with publishers, who for several years either ignored him or offered only paltry sums (sometimes never paid) for a handful of stories and articles, the first of them appearing in 1874. His hard-headedness in later dealings with publishers like Victor Havard, when he had finally become a highly marketable author, is not necessarily a sign of obstinate Norman avarice, but rather of wanting to be rewarded at his full worth by businessmen whose profits came from acting as intermediaries between an artist and his public (Havard's reluctance to pay accounts on time and distribute Maupassant's books more widely is a constant complaint in their correspondence).

Letters to his mother reveal how bleak and solitary his obscure existence was at times in the 1870s, particularly in winter, thus on 6 October 1875 he wrote: 'It's December which terrifies me, the black month, the sinister month, the deep month, the midnight of the year.'[9] Consequently, Maupassant's athletic activities in this decade deserve more exploration, because they formed a central, compensatory part of his personality. They included hiking, shooting, fencing, hunting and swimming, all of them demanding

Maupassant in hunting attire, photographed by Eugène Renouard before 1890.

physical prowess and willingness to confront danger. However, the more sedentary Flaubert chides him in August 1878 for wasting his time rowing and fornicating with rowdy companions along the banks of the river Seine, rather than honing his verses and tales in a solitary garret (Maupassant shares a chaster version of his sporting exploits with his mother). In Flaubert's opinion, 'civilized man doesn't need as much locomotion as the doctors pretend. You were born to write poetry: write it!'[10] Maupassant's first published books were indeed a slim collection of verse in 1880, preceded by a short play in 1879. Writing poems conferred a certain prestige, while plays that achieved successful theatrical performances could be lucrative; but Maupassant's contribution to these genres was unremarkable, as he soon realized.

In fact the sportsmen's camaraderie he enjoyed in the rustic environment which still existed in the villages on the outskirts of Paris gave him temporary release from the crushing tedium of weekday bureaucratic imprisonment. The *canotiers* (oarsmen) who shared cheap rooms, boats and girlfriends were only weekend bohemians: nearly all of Maupassant's intimate male friends shared his bourgeois background and later took up respectable careers. For all their promiscuous heterosexual adventures with working-class young women, whose meagre legitimate earnings made semi-prostitution a virtual necessity, the group was bound by blatantly homoerotic initiation ceremonies and exhibitionism (these involved mutual masturbation, sodomy and transvestism). Maupassant had no great sympathy for male homosexuality and passes off these macho antics as what he calls 'la farce' – that is, practical joking as a sort of metaphysical protest, an antidote to the circumscribed monotony of daily living, albeit taken to rather excessive extremes. He records for example that one unfortunate initiate actually died after enduring the group's mistreatment, adding callously 'He was a loss to nobody.'[11] In her authoritative biography, Marlo Johnston notes that the man actually died in the ministry office six months

Gustave Flaubert, Maupassant's mentor, in the late 1870s.

later (February 1880), perhaps from other causes.[12] But Maupassant and Robert Pinchon certainly did compose an obscene farce set in a brothel, *A la feuille de rose, maison turque*, which they and friends performed privately twice in April 1875 and May 1877 before a select audience; all the female parts were taken by men in drag adorned with hideously deformed genitalia. Among those present, Flaubert thought it hilarious; Edmond de Goncourt recorded his disgust at such shameless breaking of taboos, although the play had no other purpose or merit.[13]

Maupassant's nostalgic story 'Mouche' (1890) wistfully recalls this unconstrained period of physical display and enjoyment as a lost youthful idyll. It is portrayed more explicitly in some of his earlier bawdy verse, such as the poem 'Une fille' (previously entitled 'Au bord de l'eau'), which despite its relative innocuousness was briefly threatened with prosecution for indecency after it appeared in the *Revue moderne et naturaliste* in November 1879. (Some far more indecent poems of his appeared in a collective 1881 anthology of pornographic verse, *Le Nouveau Parnasse satyrique*, published more discreetly in Belgium.) But the brothel culture of easy, mercenary sex and obscene, laddish pranks in which he indulged exuberantly, and later explored more soberly in innumerable stories, would bring his destruction. In a notorious letter to Robert Pinchon dated 2 March 1877, Maupassant declares 'I've got the pox! At last! The real thing!! . . . the great pox, which Francis 1st died of.'[14] This display of juvenile bravado (syphilitic infection seen as a rite of passage, the ultimate initiation ceremony to manhood, shared by kings and poets alike) demonstrates Maupassant's perhaps fortunate ignorance of the horrendous long-term consequences of the disease.

The remaining sixteen years of his life would be troubled by increasingly severe health problems, whose intermittence and diversity (ranging from hair loss, migraine, partial blindness to digestive problems and hallucinations) mystified both author and the innumerable doctors whom he consulted ever more desperately. Maupassant's younger brother Hervé offered him a grim premonition of his own fate. Hervé shared Guy's coarser physical appetites but lacked his literary and intellectual talents, business sense and generosity. He married after leaving the army, and fathered a daughter, but failed to establish himself in a viable profession, sponging shamelessly off his mother and brother. In February 1888, after Hervé's behaviour to his family became yet more disruptive and violent, Guy wrote to him in an angrily paternal tone: 'For ten years, I've only had cause to suffer through you and to look after you, without your even being aware of this. Now I'm trying to save your life.'[15] This meant removing the unwilling Hervé to a care home; in August 1889 he was indeed forcibly detained in a psychiatric hospital in Lyon, where he died in a state of paralytic insanity three months later, aged only 33.

Hervé's disease was somewhat implausibly attributed by the family to sunstroke, and by some doctors to an unspecified hereditary weakness, thus suggesting a possible link with Guy's subsequent descent into madness. Both brothers predeceased their parents, who lived to a respectable old age, never acknowledging the true cause of their sons' deaths, which was almost certainly tertiary syphilis, acquired from sexual intercourse with an infected prostitute (their maternal uncle Alfred Le Poittevin probably also died from the same cause). In the late nineteenth century, the disease was incurable (causing at least 30,000 deaths annually in France) and its pathology poorly understood. Maupassant was probably given highly toxic treatment with mercury and potassium iodine for unpleasant secondary symptoms around 1876–7, but in many cases this failed to eradicate the microbial agent, the spirochete *Treponema pallida* (discovered only in 1905), which continued surreptitiously to attack the central nervous system and major organs, sometimes for a period of many years. The paralysis of eye muscles, together with degeneration of the optic nerve and related migraines, from which Maupassant suffered from the 1880s (forcing him to use ether as a painkiller and to employ a secretary who acted as an amanuensis and reader), is a common symptom.[16] But Maupassant and his doctors preferred to link his illnesses to a variety of nebulous causes, such as nervous exhaustion, and to follow modish but ineffective palliative treatments (such as spa cures and ice-cold showers delivered with a pressure hose). Nor does syphilis reappear in his correspondence after 1877, and it features significantly in only one story ('Le Lit 29'), which shows a heroic prostitute deliberately infecting the German soldiers who raped her. The fear of insanity, on the other hand, is an almost obsessive theme throughout his stories from 1875.

Maupassant's youthful sexual promiscuity and exhibitionism thus had very negative long-term consequences, cutting short his creative vitality and ending his life in early middle age. Given accounts by witnesses like Edmond de Goncourt and Frank Harris of his alleged fondness for demonstrating his sexual prowess in brothels, it may seem paradoxical to observe that we actually know very little about the author's love life, if we take this to mean intimate relations with specific women. This is mainly because, as the author of a book entitled *La Vie érotique de Guy de Maupassant* is obliged to admit, he was 'extremely reluctant to share confidences about his private life'.[17] Although he acknowledged his illnesses more openly, he repressed all understanding of the terrible underlying cause, even from himself. Once he became a respectable writer and a *mondain* in the early 1880s (interacting socially with wealthy and powerful members of the ruling elite and drawing most of his readers from this class), he was bound to follow conventions of absolute discretion, however much these are mocked as hypocritical duplicity in his writing. This included, for example, renting a second small apartment in Paris, presumably for clandestine encounters with ladies unable to meet him in his main residence or public places.

Another biographer remarks rather oddly that 'Guy appears to have been a sensitive and rather sceptical lover,'[18] since the little evidence we have suggests that he was exuberantly frank about sexual pleasure, at least until his health deteriorated. Some of his letters around 1881 to the bisexual 'androgyne' Gisèle d'Estoc, for example, enthusiastically record heterosexual and lesbian couplings, with Maupassant encouraging her to dress as a schoolboy and procuring ladies eager to enjoy her charms. Gisèle (whose real name was Paule Parent-Desbarres) however was a free-spirited bohemian, whose flamboyant (but ultimately intolerable) behaviour set her outside respectable society. In 1884 he claimed that he had received dozens of anonymous letters from other female admirers over the previous two years, although what then transpired usually remains unclear. In some cases at least, there was neither a meeting of minds nor bodies. For example, far from being seductive or salacious, his exchanges with Marie Bashkirtseff (a cultured but sickly young woman whom he never met and whose identity he never learned) strike an off-putting, world-weary tone, with the writer asserting, unromantically:

I don't have an ounce of poetry in me. I regard everything with indifference and I spend two-thirds of my time in profound boredom. The remaining third I occupy by writing lines which I sell for as much as possible, while regretting being obliged to pursue such an abominable profession.

Life in general is summed up in a despondent aphorism: 'Everything amounts to boredom, farce and misery.'[19]

One might deduce from this that Maupassant's hard-won prosperity and renown had merely increased his innate pessimism. But we need also to bear in mind that world-weary, cynical indifference was a defensive posture which he adopted when faced with naive or intrusive correspondents and acquaintances, having no desire to expose his personal views, feelings and suffering to celebrity-hunting busybodies. Similarly, the provocative or potentially offensive opinions which he expressed in some newspaper articles may well have been exaggerated or simplified to appeal to the particular readership of a given periodical. When it comes to his fiction, the distancing process is often still more problematic, part of an aesthetic strategy that may deceive ingenuous readers eager to 'identify' with an author and his creations. In practice, while it is usually clear that imaginary characters and the narrators who present them are not simply the author's spokespersons, deciding where the author's sympathies lie requires a subtle analysis of the overall narrative economy of a story or novel. This whole question of perspectives and judgements will be explored more specifically in subsequent chapters.

Certainly Maupassant was sceptical and sensitive about his position as a famous writer (calling himself a 'marchand de prose' in 1889, but one whose talent was genuine and itself a saleable product), whereas in sexual relations he was probably as pragmatically businesslike as he was in dealing with publishers. He told an unknown correspondent in 1890 that 'I am absolutely devoid of physical modesty, but excessively modest about feelings.'[20] Although he was rigorously commercial in deriving the maximum financial benefit from selling his writing on the most favourable terms to a wide range of periodicals and book publishers (often recycling the same material in different outlets to meet pressing deadlines), he also imposed a rigorous discipline upon himself, which put writing at the core of his life, as a primary or primordial activity. This involved withdrawing from routine social contacts in order to fulfil the voluminous production to which he was committed. Thus he reminds Victor Havard in 1881: 'I have adopted as an absolute rule never to lunch out, in order to devote the whole day to work; and a single interruption in my working habits completely throws me off track.' Nine years later, he reiterates to Dr Henri Cazalis that he needs the 'security given by the certainty that my door is barred', that 'Nobody in the world, not even my father, may enter my house in the morning.'[21] Guarding his privacy also meant declining interviews and attempting to ban the publication of his image, although he was aware that this was hardly an optimal marketing strategy (and eventually rescinded the ban to allow Nadar to sell his famous photographs).

Although in some journalistic pieces he affected to despise women for their lack of intelligence and trivial sentimentality, Maupassant nonetheless befriended and charmed a small group of sophisticated women, while carefully guarding the secrets of their intimacy. Most of them were married, highly cultivated and came from wealthy backgrounds. Whereas he derided the vanity and stupidity of the high-life snobs he encountered in Cannes (disobligingly comparing the Prince of Wales to a Norman pig dealer who looked like his animals[22]), these ladies were treated more respectfully. For several years, as Maupassant's eyesight deteriorated, Clémence Brun played a vital part in his production by acting as an unpaid secretary, but why she worked for no material reward is unknown (she was divorced and she remarried when Maupassant died). (How much of his intimate correspondence to Clem and others was posthumously culled by his mother is also unknown.) His dealings with Countess Potocka, Marie Kann, Mme Straus (Bizet's widow) and Hermine Lecomte du Noüy show an unaccustomed deference, a romantic gallantry which may have been rewarded. Hermine had no scruples about using his name to sell her books after his death. All we know for sure is that Maupassant never married, never acknowledged a *maîtresse en titre*, and apparently died childless, leaving his estate to his parents and niece. Ten years after his death, a woman called Joséphine Litzelmann asserted that Maupassant had fathered three unrecognized children with her in the 1880s. In 1904 his closest surviving friend Robert Pinchon noted the improbability of this claim: for example, all the material evidence substantiating his paternity had (in)conveniently vanished in a burglary, somewhat fancifully attributed to Maupassant's eighty-year-old mother. Some modern biographers nevertheless uncritically embrace these illegitimate children, on the grounds that the writer's many fictions dealing with bastards abandoned by their biological fathers are a clear sign of his guilty conscience.[23]

Some early biographers even asserted that Maupassant himself was the illegitimate son of another Gustave, namely his mentor Flaubert, who remained on affectionate terms with Guy and his mother until his sudden death in 1880. But again no material evidence supports such romantic inventions (even though many *ménages à trois* appear in Maupassant's fiction). Although Maupassant learned a great deal about literary writing from Flaubert (particularly concerning stylistic precision and meticulous objective presentation), their literary careers diverged significantly, making them quite different writers. Private means allowed Flaubert to travel extensively in his youth, spending nearly two years (1849–51) in North Africa and the Middle East, before he then devoted himself for three decades to producing a handful of masterly novels, each laboriously researched and composed over several years. Flaubert despised journalism and popularity; he published only three short stories towards the end of his life (when he had impoverished himself by imprudent family business investments and was humiliatingly forced to seek a state pension with Maupassant's help).

Unlike either his father or his mentor, on the other hand, Maupassant was financially astute and willing and able to exploit the expanding literary marketplace of the 1870s and '80s, using his growing popularity and extraordinary creative energy to increase both his social and economic capital (that is, his personal prestige and wealth).[24] He computed his rapidly expanding earnings with careful satisfaction, adopting an increasingly opulent bachelor lifestyle throughout the 1880s. The year before he quit the Education Ministry in June 1880, his annual salary was 2,400 francs and he could not afford a second-class return train ticket costing 36 francs from Paris to Rouen (which in our age of cheap mass travel may indeed seem a phenomenal sum for such a relatively short journey). His early newspaper articles earned him 50 francs each, but his regular contract with the daily newspaper *Le Gaulois* for a weekly article or story from May 1880 (which lasted until 1888) earned him 6,000 francs annually, and allowed him to negotiate similar rates with *Gil Blas* and other publications. He sold the serial rights of his first novel, *Une Vie*, to *Gil Blas* for 8,000 francs in 1883 (earning a further 2,000 francs for the Russian translation). With book publishers like Havard, Maupassant typically agreed royalties of 40 centimes per copy for the first 3,000 copies sold, increasing thereafter to 1 franc per copy. A book that sold 12,000 copies would thus earn him about 10,000 francs. Although such sales may seem rather modest to twenty-first-century readers used to inexpensive mass-produced paperbacks and other disposable consumer goods, in a more austere age where books were luxury items affordable only to the wealthy (a novel cost 3 francs and 50 centimes, the equivalent of about £42 today), they made him one of the best-selling authors of the day.[25] As his output and sales accumulated, his income correspondingly rose: to around 35,000 francs annually in the mid-1880s and far more by the end of the decade.

During his final decade, Maupassant lived extravagantly, maintaining several residences simultaneously (a house called La Guillette which he owned in Étretat, a lavish rented apartment in central Paris, and rented flats and houses in Cannes and other holiday villages) and successively owning two touring yachts both called *Bel-Ami* (after his 1885 novel), all of them requiring furnishings, fittings and a retinue of paid staff. This probably explains why in 1895, two years after his death, his residual estate was estimated at only 186,000 francs (about £2.2 million today).

In addition, he travelled widely in France, Italy and North Africa, leading a nomadic, restless existence while still writing and publishing prodigiously, but after 1885 he shifted his repertoire away from ephemeral articles and short tales towards more substantial novellas and novels (publishing five novels and two travel books in addition to nine story collections between 1885 and 1890).

His three travel books skilfully blend previously published newspaper pieces into more reflective, coherent narratives. Some biographers have diagnosed Maupassant's constant voyaging, from his first visits to Corsica and Algeria in 1880–81 to his final trips to Italy and Tunisia in autumn 1889 and Algeria in autumn 1890, as a form of dromomania – that is, a manic, pathological restlessness, recalling perhaps the philosopher Pascal's gloomy dictum that humanity's woes stem from our inability to remain in one place.[26] A more sympathetic interpretation (and one more plausible to modern readers living in our cosmopolitan age of mass travel and global migration) would be that Maupassant, who perceived himself as both an amateur ethnologist and a primitive being attuned to natural impulses, was rediscovering humanity's primeval, nomadic past. On a more mundane level, Maupassant himself observes, in an 1885 essay called 'Fin de saison', that 'real Parisians are never in Paris': rather like migratory birds, the wealthy and fashionable have a seasonal routine that sends them cyclically from the capital to their spas, hunting lodges and villas on the Riviera.[27]

Maupassant attributes his own urge to travel to intellectual, spiritual and physical reasons. He writes in *Au soleil* (In the Sun, 1884) that 'Any residence where one lives for long becomes a prison', whereas travel opens the door to a new, transformed life, part dream and part reality.[28] As this book's title suggests, for all his visceral attachment to Normandy and the river Seine, Maupassant's intolerance of the cold and his failing health meant that the torrid heat of Mediterranean countries was needed to make life bearable.

Such reflections are repeated and deepened in *Sur l'eau* (1888), his most overtly autobiographical book, where like Baudelaire (the poet he most admired), Maupassant alternates between depicting the horrors of life and celebrating its ecstasies. He insists on his own duality: not merely the *dédoublement* of the writer, who lives, observes and records experience concurrently, but an atavistic pantheism that detaches him from civilized beings:

> I feel stirring within me something of all species of animals,
> all instincts, all the confused desires of inferior creatures.
> I love the earth as they do, and unlike you, oh men, I love
> it without admiration, with poetry, without exaltation.
> I love with a bestial, profound love, one both despicable
> and sacred, everything that lives, that grows, that one sees.[29]

In consequence, he had no great sympathy for French colonialism, which he depicted as unjust, inefficient and unlikely to exert any civilizing influence on its dispossessed Arab and Berber subjects (while admiring the courage and enterprise of European colonial settlers and soldiers). But while Maupassant observed with cool sympathy the poverty and misery inflicted on the masses in both France and Africa by the politicians and capitalists of Western civilization, he had no desire to be a social reformer or prophet (unlike, say, Victor Hugo or Tolstoy). His encapsulation of himself as a faun (in a letter to Gisèle d'Estoc) is a further rejection of humanity: the writer as bestial man-goat, but also as mythic semi-divinity.[30]

Maupassant's final years were, however, not merely all too human, but eventually inflicted a wretched and demeaning diminution to sub-human dementia, as the light of reason was extinguished and he shared the fate to which he had consigned his more abject characters. Towards the end of 1890, he became unable to write any more than short notes, which record his irreversible mental and physical decline with stoical lucidity for another year. To Dr Cazalis in January 1891: 'I assure you that I am losing my mind. I am becoming mad. I spent yesterday evening at Princess Mathilde's, struggling for words, unable to speak, remembering nothing.' By December 1891: 'I am absolutely lost . . . Death is imminent and I am mad. Farewell, my friend, you will see me no more.'[31] During the night of 1–2 January 1892, while residing in Cannes, Maupassant cut his throat with a paper knife, but was saved by his manservant and sailors. A few days later, he was transferred to Dr Blanche's clinic in Passy, where he survived another eighteen months, perhaps thanks to his robust constitution, but in a state of increasing mental incapacity, with bouts of insomnia and manic loquacity eventually followed by epileptic convulsions, until he lapsed into a coma a few days before his death on 6 July 1893.

As we have seen, Maupassant was admired and liked by his readers and personal friends and associates, who mourned him sincerely. His loyal factotum François Tassart published an informative and affectionate memoir of his master in 1911 (with the unacknowledged assistance of Maupassant's friends Cazalis and Case). But the author's literary peers were often less respectful or sympathetic. Even admirers like Henry James and other eminent Victorians affected maidenly dismay at Maupassant's cynicism and naturalism. Early bowdlerized translations of his books were in fact banned in England for alleged obscenity, along with Zola's, and his unfortunate publisher Vizetelly was imprisoned in 1889. In 1904 Joseph Conrad dourly remarked that Maupassant's 'talent is not exercised for the praise and consolation of mankind', while Edmond de Goncourt predictably condemned his facility and commercialism.[32] Even in 1942 his biographer Paul Morand affirmed with extraordinary condescension that Maupassant had 'a somewhat vulgar nature, a lucid but limited intelligence, few artistic gifts. He owes his conscientious craftsmanship to

Édouard Manet, *Émile Zola*, 1868, oil on canvas.

Flaubert.'[33] At least five other writers among his contemporaries sought to exploit and subvert Maupassant's renown more covertly by presenting highly unflattering portraits of characters based on him in their novels – namely, Bloy, Champsaur, Lecomte du Noüy, Lorrain and Zola. With the notable exception of Zola, Maupassant's posthumous reputation and readership have far outlived this particular quintet, whose names are nowadays known only to academic specialists.

In fact, throughout the twentieth century, his sales and popularity grew exponentially, not merely in France but throughout the world. According to the French Ministry of Culture in 1999, Maupassant was placed in the top ten favourite writers of fifteen- to twenty-year-olds.[34] The culture section of *Le Figaro* on 14 March 2012 reported that Maupassant was the best-selling classic French author for 2004–11, with cumulative sales of 3.8 million copies, earning 11 million euros, ahead of Molière, Camus and Hugo (which suggests that annual sales in France of his books run to around 500,000 copies).[35] But this enduring appeal to juveniles, schoolteachers and ordinary readers merely reinforced the disdain of highbrow mid-twentieth-century commentators like Morand, who took it as further evidence of the writer's mercenary zeal, his coarse immaturity and bland superficiality, in a period where the gnomic obscurities of symbolism and the disrupted narratives of modernism often dictated critical fashions. That Maupassant's accessibility and lucidity were achieved by dedicated artistry and actually reveal subtlety, sensitivity and insight was however recognized from the outset by less partial critics prepared to study his writing on its own terms (such as the influential review editor Ferdinand Brunetière in the 1890s). From the 1950s, academic critics and researchers began at last to take Maupassant seriously, with André Vial's illuminating *Guy de Maupassant et l'art du roman* (The Art of the Novel, 1954) spawning hundreds of theses and monographs across the world in subsequent decades.

What then does Maupassant have to offer twenty-first-century readers? Contrary to Conrad's assertion, reading Maupassant is often a beguiling and pleasurable experience. His tragic personal fate and pessimism are subsumed by the literary texts, which outlive their biographical author and will presumably survive as long as Western civilization preserves cultural artefacts that connect us to the past. Above all, at his best, Maupassant absorbs us in a rich social and sensual world, presented with dexterous detail and accuracy, and driven by exciting human dramas and conflicts, in a way that is emotionally, aesthetically and intellectually satisfying. Very few other writers of fiction achieve all these goals so skilfully. In the following chapters, we will look more closely at the historical, cultural context which allowed him to thrive as a journalist and follow how he made the transition to fiction, before studying his most famous stories and novels and their underlying philosophy.

2

Journalist

Journalism made Maupassant a successful and well-rewarded writer. It liberated him from the soul-destroying drudgery inflicted on the anonymous mass of impoverished bureaucrats and transformed him into a minor celebrity, recognized by social elites as an entertaining chronicler and aspiring artist, and able to enjoy their privileged lifestyle. As we saw, this transition from obscurity to fame was a lengthy process, demanding immense dedication and patience. Between 1875 and 1879, Maupassant published only a handful of articles and stories in the press and one short play; it was finally in 1880 that his contract to produce a weekly story or essay for the daily *Le Gaulois* boosted his income sufficiently for him to quit the hated ministry. From this point onwards, Maupassant joined the relatively small group of professional men of letters who lived principally or entirely by writing and derived a substantial part of their income from publishing in the press. His contemporaries included novelists like Zola, Jules Vallès and Octave Mirbeau, literary critics like Ferdinand Brunetière and Jules Lemaître, as well as more ephemeral figures like Paul Ginisty and Aurélien Scholl. There were however far more journalists employed in the Parisian and provincial press whose lack of talent, energy or luck condemned them to much the same ill-paid toil and anonymity as the petty officials from whose ranks Maupassant had at last escaped.

Although the press brought him wealth, prestige and popularity, Maupassant was well aware of its constraints and shortcomings.

Maupassant in his prime, in the mid-1880s.

While he was generally careful to follow the editorial line and tone of the journals in which his essays, novels and stories appeared, and to avoid criticizing editors and fellow contributors in print, he resented both the relentless textual production and self-censorship which journalism required. Eventually, as these pressures grew more irksome, he withdrew from *Gil Blas* in December 1887 and threatened legal action against *Le Figaro* for cutting his essay on

'Le Roman' in January 1888. He informed Brunetière in August 1889 that his aim was to stop ephemeral journalistic writing in favour of 'a few select publications', such as the conservative but lucrative *Revue des deux mondes* (a review which he had previously scorned, until his friend Brunetière became a senior editor).[1] In more general terms of public morality, his novel *Bel-Ami* (1885) is a caustic satire of press venality and corruption; its historical accuracy and relevance also make it a fascinating document for anyone interested in the rise of the mass media. Far from offering impartial information and disinterested analysis to the reading public, the novel shows the press to be manipulated by a clique of dishonest politicians and financiers in order to further their own interests.

The influential critic and editor Ferdinand Brunetière: engraving by Charles Ogereau.

The book was serialized in *Gil Blas*, although this newspaper was in fact one of Maupassant's main targets. The obvious resemblance between fact and fiction led him to publish a half-hearted denial, entitled 'Aux critiques de *Bel-Ami*' (*Gil Blas*, 7 June 1885), in which he claimed that his unscrupulous hero Duroy was not a proper journalist and that the 'immense republic' of the press certainly contained some honest men.[2] In other words, it is tempting to conclude that Maupassant despised the press, while somewhat cynically using it as a platform from which to profit.

Apart from his fictional writing, Maupassant published more than 250 articles in French newspapers and reviews between 1876 and 1891. With the exception of the articles which he revised for his three travel books, most of them never reappeared in books, unlike his novels and most of his stories. Although he clearly valued them less than his literary writing, these press articles collectively represent a very substantial body of work, which remained unknown to many of his readers and critics until they were posthumously reassembled and published by Maupassant scholars like René Dumesnil and Gérard Delaisement. Indeed Delaisement's complete 2003 edition with its copious annotation runs to 1,854 pages.[3] While some articles are relatively trivial and repetitious, most are well written, perceptive and entertaining; they offer surprising insights into the author, his opinions and knowledge, and the underlying attitudes and assumptions of his age. Before investigating this material in detail, it is helpful to provide some broader contextual information about the press and publishing in late nineteenth-century France.

The vast expansion of the press and its readership from the 1880s to the Second World War is attributable to a nexus of social, political and economic causes. The reorganization and growth of primary education from the 1830s extended literacy beyond urban elites, eventually creating a mass audience for the popular newspapers that were founded from the 1860s onwards. For most of the nineteenth-century rural population, newspapers were the only source of information about the contemporary external world. While reading books and journals still remained a minority phenomenon and often depended on visual or auditory support (such as pictures or reading aloud to a family or community), the press helped construct a new reading culture. The serialization of episodic, melodramatic novels in newspapers such as *La Presse* and *Le Siècle* in effect created a new genre of accessible fiction (the *feuilletons* which the critic Sainte-Beuve disparaged as 'industrial literature' in 1839, anticipating similar highbrow objections to Maupassant a generation later). These were sold by individual numbers rather than expensive subscriptions, with the result that overall sales of Parisian daily newspapers doubled between 1836 and 1845 to 148,000. The *fait divers* was another creation of nineteenth-century journalism, a term which oddly has no direct equivalent in English but refers to sensational human-interest narratives or true-life *stories* (in journalistic parlance), typically involving a horrendous crime, accident or other scandalous event recounted in a voyeuristic and prurient manner. Other regular rubrics were established like the *critique* or *chronique* (that is, reviews and features articles by well-known figures), which made the press a key intermediary between the public and marketable cultural products (many such articles were in fact disguised advertising). On the other hand, news reporting as we understand it (that is, more objective information about major political and current events and issues) only became a primary function of the popular press in France from the turn of the twentieth century.

Until the Third Republic was definitively established in the late 1870s as a relatively democratic parliamentary regime, the French press suffered from severe political and economic restraints. Under the Second Empire of Napoleon III, newspapers and reviews which criticized the government or offended public morality were prosecuted and writers and editors deemed culpable were often fined or imprisoned (witness the jailing of Victor Hugo's sons and the prosecution of Baudelaire and Flaubert during this regime). Political censorship and the payment of a caution were removed in 1881, although the liberalization of the law had some negative consequences. For example, there were few restraints on publishing libels and insults, which explains the violent polemical tone of some newspapers and the frequency of duels as a means of redress. However, the offence of outraging public morality was re-introduced in 1882 (ostensibly to deter pornographers but in practice discouraging any sexually explicit representation) and the repressive laws known as the *lois scélérates* were imposed in 1893–4 to quash anarchist and terrorist propaganda in anarchist and libertarian journals.

From the 1860s, small-format Parisian dailies like *Le Petit Journal* – which sold for 5 centimes (a third of the price of more upmarket newspapers), were pitched at a broad readership, were politically neutral and thus exempt from stamp duty, and quicker and cheaper to print – rapidly captured most of the market. By 1914 the four most-popular French daily newspapers were printing 5 million copies. In the closing decades of the century, an abundance of capital and speculation promoted new titles (and corruption by vested interests), while technical progress in printing and distribution cut costs and prices. By 1897 there were 5,787 periodicals being published in France, covering a vast range of specialized interests. The generalist daily press was increasingly bound to market laws and to appeal to the particular prejudices of its readership, whereas in earlier decades newspapers took a more overtly political stance (typically for or against the regime in power).[4] This explains the largely negative role played by the French press in the Dreyfus Affair in the years immediately after Maupassant's death. The Affair was effectively launched as a public scandal when the nationalist press leaked news of the Jewish officer Dreyfus' conviction for espionage in November 1894 (the organ involved, *La Libre Parole*, was actually closely associated with the real culprit Esterhazy). But most of the press followed this newspaper's lead, preferring anti-Semitic denunciation to investigating the truth and thereby 'maintaining a culture of lying, forgery, rumours, conformism and anti-intellectualism'.[5] Only newspapers and reviews read by the liberal elite, less than 10 per cent of the public, were prepared to expose and challenge the army and government's duplicity, by actively promoting the case for Dreyfus' innocence. Within two decades, the hard-won freedom of the popular press was being abused to bamboozle the masses with sensational fantasies and racist slanders.

Many other examples of press venality from the *fin-de-siècle* could be cited, which certainly reaffirm the prescience of Maupassant's critical depiction of journalism in *Bel-Ami* (such as revelations that major newspaper editors had taken substantial bribes to promote the failing Panama canal company or to conceal the Ottoman Sultan's massacre of Armenians, apart from the more routine malfeasance of financial journalists and theatre and book reviewers deriving from the interdependence of press, finance and producers). The influential *Revue bleue* in fact launched a critical debate in 1897–8 about the manifest shortcomings of the French press, which were linked to a supposed crisis in state institutions (most notably illustrated by the Dreyfus Affair). However, Thomas Ferenczi argues that a less partial analysis reveals the positive, democratic influence exercised by at least some sectors of the French press: its growing plurality meant that many of these abuses were actually revealed by rival newspapers or more independent journalists.[6]

Nevertheless, around 1900, the Parisian press was viewed internationally as an important cultural medium, but one that produced and promoted entertainment and artistic talent rather than disinterested information or professional journalism. Journalism as an independent profession (with vocational training, ethics, pensions and other benefits) was established only in the early twentieth century. Most successful nineteenth-century French journalists were talented amateurs, like Maupassant. As *Bel-Ami* demonstrates, unlike careers in the arts, sciences and professions demanding studious training and expertise, journalism primarily requires verbal fluency, self-confidence and skilful networking. Writing successful *chroniques* (that is, attracting readers and boosting sales) necessitated an appealing spontaneity and facility, although despite its skilful packaging the output might soon look ephemeral and superficial. A star *chroniqueur* like Aurélien Scholl (whom Maupassant tactfully praised) was already outmoded by the 1880s (and his police dossier also reveals convictions for assault, indecent behaviour, libel and embezzlement).[7] For the most able, journalism could be a bridge to a more respectable career as a critic, novelist or playwright, or in public service (for example, launching Clemenceau as a politician and Ginisty as a theatre director).

Most generalist newspapers devoted a lot of space to serialized fiction and cultural articles, whatever their readership. For example, Fernand Xau's *Le Journal* was launched in 1892 as a literary paper costing 5 centimes specifically aimed at shopkeepers, workers, primary school teachers and clerks; by 1914 it was selling 1 million copies daily.[8] Nearly all of Maupassant's articles and fiction first appeared in more costly Parisian periodicals aimed at a less plebeian readership (although he reissued some stories in more popular or provincial newspapers). In fact he published 204 of his articles (about 82 per cent of his known output) in the two cultural dailies *Le Gaulois* and *Gil Blas* (as he did with his stories).

Like most nineteenth-century French newspapers, these two journals (now accessible digitally via the Bibliothèque Nationale website) bear little resemblance to the daily press of either the twentieth or twenty-first centuries. Both were published in tabloid format, with six densely packed columns in barely readable print on each of their four pages, and sold for 15 centimes in Paris and

20 centimes elsewhere (the equivalent of about £2 in 2019). The issue published on 1 January 1885 of the more conservative *Le Gaulois* (founded in 1868, it sold about 25,000 copies in the mid-1880s and survived until the 1920s) offers New Year best wishes to the comte de Paris (the royalist pretender) on its first page, followed by political and miscellaneous news on pages one and two; page three is filled by theatre reviews and a serialized novel, with advertisements and stock exchange reports on the last page. Though similar in appearance, on the same date *Gil Blas* (founded in 1879, it sold about 28,000 copies and lasted until the financial crisis triggered by the outbreak of war in 1914) has a front page containing a story and snippets of gossip, with miscellaneous information and news on page two, sport and an episode of Zola's novel *Germinal* on page three, and a final page containing advertisements, and reports on theatrical shows and the stock exchange. *Gil Blas* was more salacious in tone than *Le Gaulois*, which is duly reflected in Maupassant's choice of material for his pieces; it was also more liable to prosecution (its gossip column was used to promote high-class prostitutes and to blackmail society figures who had committed indiscretions).[9] Despite their relatively modest sales, these newspapers paid writers well for serial rights, allowing them to reach a far bigger audience and earn far more than they would from book sales alone (where sales of 3,000 copies or less were typical).

Most of Maupassant's journalistic articles in these two newspapers are *chroniques*, that is, discursive, essayistic pieces of about 2,500 words offering the writer's personal views and observations on current affairs and a vast range of cultural topics. This personal, non-fictional core distinguishes them from most of his stories, which are fictional narratives about invented people, often recounted by narrators whose perspective and judgements differ significantly from the author's. Occasionally, the boundary between fact and fiction is unclear. For example, an episode from Bonaparte's early career, 'Une page d'histoire inédite' (*Le Gaulois*, 27 October 1880), appears in posthumous anthologies of both his journalism and his stories, though Maupassant never republished it. The word *histoire* thus retains its generic ambiguity: this narrative may be unrecorded history, or just a fanciful story. In any event, some caution is always needed in determining the author's standpoint and implied opinion when an article deals with contentious issues. Obfuscation or concealment may suit him better than overt pronouncements. For contractual reasons, his earlier pieces in *Gil Blas* appeared under a (transparent) pseudonym; in other potentially controversial cases, he sometimes assigned the article (for example, articles critical of French colonial policy in North Africa) to a fictitious witness or author. Moreover, as we have already seen, a successful article has to please the readers and editors of the journal in which it is published, which means adopting a style, rhetoric and ideological position in accord with this particular conservative, privileged audience (whose views and attitudes are unlikely to correspond to those of most twenty-first-century readers in areas like social equality, women's rights and sexuality).

Ironically, some twenty-first-century readers are perhaps more likely to be shocked than Maupassant's contemporaries on sampling a few of his more provocative essays, for they may find them distastefully reactionary.[10] The political correctness which has infected the Western media and education system for the last four decades tends to encourage naively anachronistic misreading of authors from the earlier twentieth century and before, periods when egalitarianism of class, race or gender was not considered either desirable or achievable. By the standards of his time, Maupassant was actually highly critical of accepted social norms and the dual standards and abuses they fostered, even if he rejects political engagement or progressive ideologies as a solution. His best articles also certainly amount to more than the opportunistic, bland entertainment that characterizes the mid-nineteenth-century *chronique*. In a series of essays on 'Les Chroniqueurs parisiens', his contemporary Jules Lemaître compared the eternal truths expressed by a poet like Lamartine with the 'literary dust', the ephemeral trivia churned out by journalists who waste their own and their readers' time on society weddings, scandals and actors' gossip.[11] In fact, after the liberalization of the press in the early 1880s, more ambitious writers were able to dispense with such whimsical frivolity and develop the *chronique* as a vehicle for serious reflection on culture, politics and philosophy.

Maupassant offered his own reflections on the genre and its practitioners in 'Messieurs de la chronique' (*Gil Blas*, 11 November 1884). He makes a clear distinction between the literary skills required by the novelist and the journalistic abilities needed to produce a readable features article, in effect implying a hierarchy of talent and value while carefully avoiding overt disparagement of his journalistic peers (a notoriously touchy breed, as he notes). He argues that the novel demands detailed observation and penetration, of people and ideas, as well as compositional coherence of thought and cohesion of events. Journalism, on the other hand, deals in the factual and short term, and the *chroniqueur* needs to display style, dash and wit rather than profundity of observation or ideas. The novelist needs stamina and artistry to create a substantial work rich in plot and the atmosphere in which its characters exist and evolve (successful novels must create their own environment and ecology, as it were). Such qualities are irrelevant in a newspaper piece, which requires little preparation, but has to be short and punchy, abruptly moving from one point to another with 'good humour, lightness, vivacity, wit and grace'. In consequence, novelists rarely if ever make good journalists, and vice versa. The productive facility required of journalists can prove exhausting in the longer term, and they are utterly dependent on the favour of a fickle public, whereas the novelist can 'defy or deride the anger of his judges and await the justice of the future'.[12]

The logic of this argument, of course, is that Maupassant's own journalistic production is ultimately incompatible with his emergent artistic ambitions to become a novelist banking his cultural capital with posterity. By November 1884 he had published only one novel (*Une Vie* in 1883, laboriously composed over many years), and was completing the second, *Bel-Ami*, published in 1885. In fact, the vast majority of his newspaper articles were published between 1880 and 1885 (with only 20 per cent appearing in the following six years from 1886 to 1891, when he published four more novels and abandoned two others). In a purely material sense, journalism was a more amenable and lucrative activity than being a government clerk; both involve information-processing and writing to order, with the obvious difference that the journalist enjoys far more creative autonomy and a far larger audience than the bureaucrat recording the routines of his ministerial hierarchy. Whatever Maupassant's longer-term reservations about journalism as an incipient profession, writing for the press provided an excellent training in observation, concision and immediacy (what Hubert Juin calls his 'gymnastics').[13] Yet while few challenge the precocious mastery of short stories and essays which Maupassant demonstrated thanks to the press, critical opinion about his six published novels has been far more divided (as a later chapter will show).

In sum, Maupassant was a skilled and versatile journalist, covering a very wide range of topics in a lucid and engaging manner (these included gourmandise, duelling, ballooning, rowing, natural history and interior decoration among many others). His skill sometimes was primarily rhetorical: it involved writing persuasively and entertainingly about subjects that may seem trivial or irrelevant to twenty-first-century readers, or dexterously exploiting the fairly superficial knowledge from which his pronouncements derived. His best writing, on the other hand, was usually based on genuine expertise and commitment or first-hand observation, demonstrated particularly in extended articles on literature (especially Flaubert) and the series of quasi-ethnographic and philosophical accounts of travel around the Mediterranean (much of this material also appeared in prefaces to books or his own travel books). Indeed he assures readers that 'the habits of life of a people, their habitual way of being, can best be grasped in the daily press, which exactly represents the intimate physiognomy of a country' ('La Politesse', *Le Gaulois*, 11 October 1881).[14] Although his views on social issues are often remote from those of twenty-first-century readers, he adopts a sceptical attitude towards the political and cultural establishment of his age, while flattering (or occasionally teasing and provoking) his targeted readers. While rejecting overt moralizing, he often provides trenchantly cynical judgements about human behaviour and destiny in the aphoristic style of French *moralistes* like La Rochefoucauld in his *Maximes* (1665). Thus arguing that human behaviour is essentially egocentric and self-deceiving ('Le Fond du coeur', 1884), Maupassant asserts 'Every human action is a manifestation of disguised egoism'; 'one loves one's neighbour on account of the good which one has done him.'[15]

The rest of this chapter and the next will illustrate and develop these points by examining specific articles and topics in more detail. Maupassant's articles began in 1876 with essays on Flaubert and Balzac (whose work he knew intimately) and ended in 1891 with a preface to a translation of Swinburne's poetry. Though he admits he cannot read English, in his youth he had briefly met the poet in Normandy. But setting aside his literary criticism until the next chapter, we will concentrate here on the most controversial areas (such as gender, social class and injustice, and the perception of humanity that underpins them), after briefly sampling some articles that show his diversity and versatility.

'Les Cadeaux' is an early article, published in *Le Gaulois* on 7 January 1881, which is ostensibly a somewhat bland review of the custom of giving New Year's presents to friends and acquaintances. On closer inspection, however, it reveals a complex nexus of social relationships and obligations, which is utterly alien to most twenty-first-century readers and presumably exclusive to the wealthier ranks of the upper bourgeoisie in *fin-de-siècle* Paris. The writer poses as a knowing (somewhat condescending) connoisseur of the salons and boudoirs belonging to the 'pretty women' whom he addresses directly as 'mesdames', while decoding the significance of the gifts lining their shelves, for these are 'always the voice of a desire'.[16] Thus jewellery is overtly sensual (other than antique pieces, it is tantamount to handing over cash for favours anticipated or granted), which is why women like it; whereas flowers are platonic. Sweets matter less than their container, since it was customary to place them inside a valuable lacquered box or porcelain ornament, costing perhaps 25 louis (500 francs, a fabulous sum), in return for the dining or other rights enjoyed by the donor. After this preamble, Maupassant changes direction and launches into a lengthy history of porcelain manufacturing from ancient China to modern Europe which occupies most of the piece (and which he unabashedly recycled the following year in *Gil Blas* as 'Vieux pots').

Two weeks later (*Le Gaulois*, 23 January 1881), with 'La Verte Érin', his subject and tone change radically. Whereas this clichéd epithet conceals the grim reality of 'this land of eternal misery, this ragged, sordid country of beggars, this homeland of endless revolt, sanguinary religion and inveterate superstition', the word 'Ireland' immediately evokes images of death, servitude and bloody struggles.[17] Although he never set foot in Ireland, Maupassant offers his readers a rapid panorama of English tyranny; the potato; brutish peasants and their swine; whiskey and the supernatural spirits evoked by its consumption; the cult of saints; funeral rites and movements for political independence. Like many adroit journalists, he omits to mention his sources, thereby implying authoritative first-hand knowledge, at least to uninformed readers who probably have no objection to unflattering and stereotyped accounts of Irish backwardness and British exploitation. On the other hand, his equally caustic and much better informed accounts of French colonialism and its abuses in Algeria published in *Le Gaulois* six months later did arouse protests from interested parties and obliged him to produce a self-justifying response ('Lettre d'Afrique', 20 August 1881). And press articles deriving from later visits to the Maghreb generally eschew the undiplomatic economic and political criticism expressed in 1881 in favour of the personal experiences and encounters with people and landscapes at which he excels.

In his articles on natural history and science, Maupassant presents himself as a rationalist and materialist: whatever the limits of our knowledge and of our mental and perceptual capacity, the chain of causality is certain and the supernatural is no longer viable; all phenomena are explicable by natural laws. He places himself firmly in the camp of those who accept scientific progress ('Adieu mystères', *Le Gaulois*, 8 November 1881), in theory at least. For if certain later stories (like 'Le Horla' and 'Qui sait?') stress the prevalence of mystery and terror, as yet inexplicable to science, in a curious article entitled 'Un miracle' (*Gil Blas*, 9 May 1886), Maupassant boldly asserts that rabies does not exist in humans, that its symptoms are neurotic and imaginary, and the supposed effectiveness of Pasteur's inoculations is purely psychosomatic. These assertions are even presented as a letter forwarded from an established provincial veterinary surgeon, in order to reinforce their authenticity. Either Maupassant is espousing the reactionary rejection of scientific discovery and innovation characteristic of so many nineteenth-century medical practitioners, or he is enjoying an elaborate hoax about a fearsome disease that was no laughing matter.[18] Pasteur began treating humans with attenuated vaccine in 1885, before the pathology of rabies was fully understood: not all those bitten by rabid animals develop the disease, and the virus became visible only with the invention of the electron microscope in 1946. However, a posthumous 1915 study of 6,000 victims vindicated Pasteur, showing that 16 per cent of unvaccinated patients died, as opposed to 0.6 per cent of vaccinated patients.[19]

Prefacing a useful paperback edition of Maupassant's *Chroniques*, Hubert Juin argues that he was a brilliant observer of his society but a highly partial commentator. This does not entirely correspond to Maupassant's dictum (derived from Flaubert's cult of *impassibilité*): 'The novelist is not a moralist; his mission is neither to correct nor modify manners and morals. His role should be restricted to observing and describing, following his temperament, according to the limits of his talent' ('Les Masques', *Gil Blas*, 5 June 1883).[20] Intrusive preaching and didacticism in literary works are aesthetically offensive (although the author's views are evidently implied by his approach to the subject chosen). Even as a journalist, Maupassant is disinclined to support a particular party, lobby or clique (he refused to become a Freemason, and scorned literary schools, academic prizes, and decorations awarded by corrupt politicians). Hence his maxim that 'the only thing that all men hate, in both religion and politics, is true independence of mind.'[21] But Juin considers the writer's independent stance to be untenable, to betray an 'anarchisme de salon', or the petty bourgeois views of *employés*, adding for good measure that Maupassant 'is entirely within the world of *rentiers*, careerists and speculators', for 'he does not write for the masses, he writes for an elite.'[22] It is true that Maupassant's critical detachment may seem hypocritical or cynical, as has already been noted. Yet Juin's disapproving argument is unpersuasive. Although he did express sympathy for revolutionary anarchists (because they reject all forms of centralized government (see 'Contemporains', *Le Gaulois*, 16 November 1881)), unlike his colleague Octave Mirbeau, Maupassant never supported anarchism (if by this we mean a radical political programme aimed at destroying the established order); and while he mixed socially with clerks and business people, he hardly shared their conservative and conventional habits and opinions (on say, marriage and the family, warfare and patriotism, or the arts and religion).

Just as he profited from and disapproved of the press, Maupassant enjoyed the benefits which society conferred on the wealthy elite, while being aware of (and moderately hostile to) the suffering and injustice inflicted on the weak and poorer classes. But he was not a social reformer (and derided reformers' antics and self-deception); a hierarchical, competitive society of winners and losers seemed entirely natural to him, provided that it fostered individual talents rather than privileges of birth. Hence his dictum that, 'Of all the foolish notions with which people are governed, *equality* is perhaps the greatest, because it is the most chimerical of utopias.' It patently does not exist in nature: 'when equality of sizes and noses has been established, I will believe in the equality of beings.' As for the more modest concept of equality before the law, he notes that it is rarely applied in practice; or if it is, it can be pernicious in its consequences. Maupassant's ire is particularly aroused by the proposal to extend a compulsory three-year term of military service to all social classes, on the grounds that its mindless drills and servile discipline will destroy the intellectual and artistic potential of the most able young men ('L'Égalité', *Le Gaulois*, 25 June 1883).[23] He thus has little sympathy for democracy and universal (male) suffrage, which give power to venal and incompetent politicians and encourage 'all sorts of ignorance, gross desires and the baseness of the uncultivated human animal' ('Danger public', *Le Gaulois*, 23 December 1889).[24]

Though he was well aware of the financial chicanery and quest for booty that characterized the internal and foreign policies of the Third Republic in the 1880s, Maupassant admitted he had no real understanding of economics and dismissed international relations as 'twaddle'.[25] He had little sense that a more accountable government might act as a positive force for peace and prosperity or that democracy and education might be a safeguard against tyranny or the dominance of vested interests. His social attitudes in these press articles are largely determined by a somewhat ingenuous aesthetic elitism (similar to that of Flaubert and Huysmans, and remote from the social engagement of Zola or Jules Vallès, or the messianic zeal of Victor Hugo and Tolstoy). Rather like Huysmans' decadent aesthete des Esseintes in À rebours (1884), he decried the popular classes' lack of taste 'in our utilitarian, uncouth society',[26] is troubled by the mindless frenzy of crowds,[27] and considers commiseration for animals the mark of an advanced society,[28] deploring the callous cruelty of peasants, and remarking that, unlike humans, animals rarely practise infanticide.[29]

The artistic elite thus has little in common with the masses:

> We do not write for the common people; we care little for what generally interests them; in truth, we are quite apart from them. Art, of whatever kind, only addresses the intellectual aristocracy of a country . . . The people, the crowd toil, struggle, suffer indeed from countless privations, precisely because they are the people, that is the barely civilized, illiterate, brutal masses. ('A propos du peuple', *Le Gaulois*, 19 November 1883)[30]

Elsewhere, Maupassant asserts that 'Art is aristocratic, therein lie its force and grandeur. To dream of popular art is mere foolishness. The higher it rises, the less it is understood by most people, but the more it is adored by those few capable of penetrating it' ('Discours académique', *Gil Blas*, 18 July 1882).[31] Were these lofty pretensions true, one might object, Maupassant himself would never have become a popular writer attracting millions of ordinary readers, a writer who actually depicts people of all classes and races with understated empathy and subtlety. His failure to anticipate the social and economic changes that within a few decades would produce a democratized mass culture no doubt reveals his limitations as a thinker, or perhaps the limits of mercenary journalism whose principal aim is to flatter complacent, blinkered elites with patronizing comments about their inferiors.

Maupassant had little knowledge of industrial workers and rarely mentions them. He briefly visited a mine, but only to draw the conclusion that miners' working conditions were no worse than those of clerks trapped all day in gloomy offices. Indeed, he concludes that this latter category is by far the most pitiable and disfavoured group of all employees ('A propos du peuple', 19 November 1883, and 'Les Employés', 4 January 1882, both in *Le Gaulois*). Since mining accidents regularly crippled or killed hundreds and cumulatively thousands of miners, well into the twentieth century, such ludicrous comments from a normally lucid and dispassionate observer are mystifying.[32] It is as if he had been so traumatized by his own unpleasant experiences in the ministry that he lost all sense of proportion in appreciating the far graver risks to which manual workers were exposed.

Some readers may make a similar judgement about Maupassant's views on women and gender, with which this chapter concludes. Here, however, ignorance is not a defence, since he knew women all too well. It is perfectly possible, by selective quotation of his more provocative utterances, to portray him as a reactionary misogynist unable to see beyond the prejudices and commonplaces of his age. This was indeed the line taken by early feminist critics until the 1940s.[33] Subsequently, more nuanced readings have stressed the ambivalence and evolution of Maupassant's attitude. Chantal Jennings, for example, stresses his duality: while he insists on women's inherent biological inferiority to men, he attacks their social oppression, paradoxically approaching a feminist viewpoint.[34]

Maupassant's views arguably evolve through three stages. First, he is never a woman-hater, being sexually and emotionally attracted to a wide range of women (while finding child-bearing and reproduction repugnant and marriage a form of imprisonment). His promiscuous sexual hunger for these 'fruits of living flesh' is frequently expressed.[35] Thus he writes in an 1883 preface that 'to keep only one woman forever would seem to me as surprising and illogical as a lover of oysters who ate only oysters at every meal, all year.'[36] Anticipating Freud, he writes that 'It is undeniable that sexual relations between men and women occupy the largest place in our lives and that they are the determining motive of most of our actions' ('Les Audacieux', *Gil Blas*, 27 November 1883).[37] Second, when he begins to articulate his opinions in his early newspaper articles, female inferiority is taken as axiomatic, with various authorities and historical cases mustered in support of this conventional position (which twenty-first-century readers probably find unconvincing and unpalatable). Finally, in the course of the 1880s, numerous counter-examples such as encounters with talented women undermine these facile assumptions, and his later fictional works often show women taking a dominant role in personal relationships.

Some characteristic illustrations should flesh out this outline. In 'La Lysistrata moderne' (*Le Gaulois*, 30 December 1880), Maupassant enumerates a series of negative judgements by male authorities, starting with Schopenhauer (while conceding these may seem exaggerated and inconclusive). Thus women's frail physique renders them incapable of demanding mental or physical work; their immature nature fits them particularly for childcare, for they are like grown-up children; women never mature intellectually beyond the age of eighteen and are incapable of abstract thought; laws according them equality are therefore absurd. Their lack of historical or artistic achievements (deemed 'irrefutable') is then added, as is Herbert Spencer's assertion that women are as incapable of intellectual labour as men are of bearing children. Yet women's capacity to please and charm has nonetheless given them immense power over men's hearts and minds, making them 'mistress of the world'. This is perhaps why Maupassant concludes this diatribe by slavishly apostrophizing his female readers and begging forgiveness for any offence he may have caused.[38]

Other articles written in 1882 develop a notion Maupassant attributes to Napoleon, that women's intelligence does not vary significantly between individuals and classes (unlike men's), but that they are remarkably adaptable to the milieu of the man to whom they are attached (so a whore can rapidly transform into a society lady).[39] Men, on the other hand, are frequently unwilling to take on women already 'used' by other men; a widow is thus 'slightly soiled goods' ('A propos du divorce', *Le Gaulois*, 27 June 1882).[40] In a preface to Prévost's classic novel about a *femme fatale*, *Manon Lescaut* (1731), he writes in 1885 that woman 'dominates and enchants man by the shape of her body, the smile on her lips and the power of her gaze', but is inconceivable in the role of a doctor or politician.[41] Sexually undesirable females (such as young girls or ageing spinsters) are barely women at all.[42] Indeed, he finds sexually active older women to be morally repugnant (comparing them to men who abuse minors), while conceding that an attractive elderly woman who retires gracefully can become a historical antique.[43]

Maupassant probably regarded such statements about gender roles as examples of sexual dimorphism, determined universally and biologically rather than by social conventions and prejudices. This perhaps explains why he is hostile to abusive practices based purely on coercion or force against subordinate beings (such as women and animals). Thus he strongly disapproves of wife-beating or husbands who kill adulterous wives, comparing the double standards of bourgeois marriage to a sentence to hard labour:

The exclusive right of ownership exercised over a being
equal to ourselves constitutes a sort of slavery, destroys
in part the free will of this being, and in any case is
certainly a flagrant assault on the integrity of her liberty
('Un dilemme', *Le Gaulois*, 22 November 1881).[44]

He considers his views on marriage and monogamy to be
'subversive', noting that adultery is commonplace among the
aristocracy, and incest as common as adultery among the lower
orders.[45] On the other hand, in an essay entitled 'L'Homme-fille'
(*Gil Blas*, 13 March 1883), he adopts a more nuanced position
towards gender-determined behaviour, if only in order to complain
that male *arrivistes* in politics and the press are 'the plague of our
country', for they behave increasingly like women. For all their
charm, they are 'changing, capricious, innocently perfidious,
inconsistent in their convictions and will, violent and weak'.[46]

When it comes to specific women whose professional success
and abilities patently contradict Maupassant's generalizing
judgements, tact and self-interest generally override orthodox
dogma, particularly when personal acquaintances are involved.
In articles on contemporary women writers, he admits that
they are unusual 'phenomena' who break gender roles (and all
the more interesting for that).[47] Influential acquaintances like
Juliette Lamber (also known as Juliette Adam, the director of *La
Nouvelle Revue*) or the actress Mme Pasca are treated somewhat
obsequiously. George Sand (Aurore Dupin, Baroness Dudevant,
famous for her romantic, pastoral novels and liaisons with
Musset and Chopin), who died in 1876 and was probably the most
influential French woman writer in the mid-century, also receives
polite treatment. Her creative energy, passion and independent
spirit made her 'a woman in whom nature had erred', defying male
superiority much as 'a socialist exasperates a king'.[48] Nonetheless,
like all female (and most male) writers, she lacks the 'divine

The influential critic and editor Juliette Adam, photographed by Nadar in 1910.

intoxication of artistic creation' enjoyed by the true creative genius.[49]

Unlike his conservative, second-hand views on women's innate inferiority (which his personal observation of marriage, family dynamics and friendships hardly supports in any case), Maupassant's conception of literary and artistic creation and craft is rather more interesting and original, since it is based on deep-seated beliefs as well as personal knowledge and practice. These merit fuller discussion in the next chapter, as does the evolution of his writing through different genres (the alternation of journalism and short fiction, the experiments with verse and drama, the desire to extend long stories into full-blown novels). To sum up this discussion, we have seen the constraints and limitations of journalism, which Maupassant was well aware of: the need to pander to editors' and readers' prejudices; the facility, expediency and recycling necessitated by production deadlines; the inherently trivial and ephemeral nature of a medium whose main aims were amusement or covert promotion (rather than objective reporting, critical insights or artistic originality). That said, there is no doubt that Maupassant was a skilful and successful journalist and that without the financial benefits, prestige and training achieved through journalism, his literary career would never have flourished. In addition, although most of his articles never appeared outside daily newspapers, the satirical and pessimistic chronicle of social and cultural life during the early Third Republic which they collectively form is transplanted and transformed in their fictional counterparts. Gérard Delaisement has shown, for example, that material from no less than fifty newspaper articles and stories is reused in *Bel-Ami*.[50] Without such novels, we would have little interest today in their author's journalism (beyond his travelogues); but without the journalism, such a richly documented, historically perceptive novel would not exist.

3

Writer

Just as his journalism was long neglected, few modern readers think of Maupassant as a poet or dramatist, although the first books he published were a verse sketch (*Histoire du vieux temps*, 1879) and a slender volume of poetry (*Des Vers*, 1880). And in fact his final book publications were also plays: *Musotte* (1891), co-authored with Jacques Normand, and *La Paix du ménage* (written before his decline, but premiered in March 1893 four months before his death). Such generic versatility was actually common among nineteenth-century writers. For example, the novelists Flaubert, Zola and Mirbeau wrote plays, while Zola, Huysmans and Mirbeau also wrote influential art criticism; they were all overshadowed by the poet Victor Hugo, whose novels and dramas survived and thrived into and beyond the twentieth century (sometimes as films and operas). While publishing poetry conferred modest literary prestige on a debutant (and required less time and energy than writing long stories and novels), successful theatrical performances were extremely lucrative, since authors usually took a percentage of the receipts. Thus the seventy performances of *Musotte* in Paris and the provinces earned Maupassant and Normand jointly 21,000 francs (selling rights to or collaborating with a professional adaptor was a common stratagem adopted by marketable authors). Why these works are now largely forgotten will be discussed later in this chapter.

Maupassant's versatility, productivity and facility during his intensely creative decade as a full-time writer certainly equal or outdo most of his contemporaries, but he left very few traces of his actual writing methods. Hence Jules Lemaître's notorious observation that Maupassant made 'masterpieces as apple trees in Normandy produce apples', as though literary creation were an involuntary, biological process not requiring conscious research, effort, composition and revision.[1] Whereas Zola and Flaubert left substantial archives that reveal a great deal about the composition and evolution of their work, no such preliminary and preparatory material survives from Maupassant (with the notable exception of his first novel, *Une Vie*). This is quite surprising, given that he clearly undertook research and collected documentation, particularly in his journalism and novels. Henri Mitterand notes for example that the wealth of factual detail that enriches the North African travelogues implies detailed note-taking on a daily basis throughout the journeys; but such notebooks have either vanished or never existed.[2] Although Maupassant actually edited Flaubert's unfinished novel *Bouvard et Pécuchet* for posthumous publication and published relevant preparatory material, he seemingly had no corresponding urge to conserve and reveal his own creative sources.

There are two possible explanations for this absence. One is that Maupassant was far more interested in the final product than the process of writing (unlike Flaubert, who had the leisure to fetishize endless research and stylistic revision). Some critics have assumed his facility and haste meant that he felt little need to undertake such preparation or revision, particularly for short articles and stories knocked out in just a few hours or days. He admitted to not checking proofs of newspaper articles and sometimes forgetfully offered the same story to different publishers. In other words, the economy of means demanded by short texts extended to their preparation. However, comparisons between surviving manuscripts and newspaper and book versions of stories and novels generally reveal that expediency did not in fact deter or prevent the writer from making corrections and other revisions to successive

Maupassant, photographed by Nadar in 1888.

versions of works, which invariably improved their organization and impact.[3]

On the other hand, a deeper psychological explanation suggests the apple tree simile is perhaps more valid than it may at first seem. Just as he concealed personal emotions and relationships from outsiders and repressed conscious awareness of the probable source of his illness, Maupassant was reluctant to probe and display the secret workings of his creativity; indeed to work properly his artistry needed to be spontaneous and involuntary.[4] Hermine Lecomte du Nouÿ claimed that he prepared books mentally for months, until finally they emerged ready-made from his pen. Similarly, his valet François observed that 'he always wrote from memory, and never had to search for long; his prodigious memory helped him a lot.' Rather like Charles Dickens, Maupassant's energetic solitary walks served as 'a sort of darkroom' in which his books were fully developed before being written.[5]

Much like his ambivalent attitude towards the press, Maupassant's association with other writers was opportunistic: cultivating them was essential, but not at the cost of surrendering his creative autonomy. When still an unknown figure, he wrote to Pinchon in February 1877: 'I belong to a literary group which disdains poetry. They will serve as a foil to me; it's a smart move.'[6] As soon as his work had attracted notice, he made clear his distrust of schools and movements, rapidly withdrawing from Zola and his acolytes after the publication of 'Boule de suif' in their collective volume *Les Soirées de Médan* in April 1880, and sending Flaubert uncomplimentary comments on his co-authors' stories. In a preface written in 1883, he remarked even more bluntly: 'I can no longer understand the classification which is established between realists, idealists, romantics, materialists and naturalists. These otiose discussions are the consolation of pedants.'[7] In the longer term, doctrines matter little, since only works will endure ('Émile Zola', 1883). In his opinion, an original writer was one who developed

Maupassant and his contemporaries (Maupassant is second left on the bottom row).

Caricature of Flaubert by Eugène Giraud, 1867.

a personal vision, 'primarily of small things and not big ones' (to Maurice Vaucaire, July 1886).

Maupassant's rejection of dogmatism and coteries also made him reluctant to criticize other contemporary writers, provided their work matched these relatively open-ended aesthetic criteria. His literary reviews and essays merit fuller analysis, because they effectively provide an oblique commentary on his own practice and technique as a writer, which the remainder of this chapter will then examine in more detail. Like Flaubert and Schopenhauer (unknowingly perhaps echoing Aristotle's *Poetics*), Maupassant makes a sharp distinction between everyday experience of objects and the complex sensations aroused by the artistic representation of an object, by the transformative power of art, whereby 'the most hideous and repugnant thing can become admirable through the brush or pen of a great artist' ('Au Salon', 30 April 1886).[8] In other words, there is no fixed hierarchy of appropriate or unsuitable subjects, but only a hierarchy of talent. A skilled interpreter can endow something that is ugly 'with a beauty independent of itself, whereas the truest and finest thought can fatally vanish within an ugly, clumsy phrase' ('Gustave Flaubert', 22 October 1876).[9]

The novelist is not a moralist charged with improving bad behaviour, but a detached, impartial observer. Accusations of obscenity and prosecutions of innovative artists who represent taboo subjects are thus unjustifiable. This argument obviously contradicts the censorious conservatism of the cultural establishment and authoritarian judiciary in mid-nineteenth-century France. Maupassant does however accept certain restraints: for example, novelists should not libel real people; even if their work is based on actual events, the real actors involved should be disguised ('Les Masques', 5 June 1883). His most interesting observations always return either to freedom of expression or to style and formal issues – that is, the qualities that distinguish good from bad writing, and endow it with ethical and artistic value. Most readers tend to confuse such qualities with bombastic rhetoric: 'the public generally understands by "form" a certain sonority of words presented in rounded periods, with imposing opening phrases and melodious endings' ('Gustave Flaubert', 22 October 1876).[10] He prefers Flaubert's more rigorous conception: style 'does not consist in a certain conventional elegance of construction, but in the absolute rightness of the word and in the perfect concord of expression with the idea expressed' ('Gustave Flaubert d'après ses lettres', 6 September 1880).[11]

The public also has a great appetite for what Maupassant calls 'idealist' literature, writing that is 'implausible, sympathetic and consoling' but fails to represent things as they really are; he rejects such pervasive hypocrisy and mendacity ('Autour d'un livre', 4 October 1881).[12] This is why he prefers Huysmans' pessimistic account in *A vau-l'eau* (1882) of petty bourgeois deprivation in the real world to Alexandre Dumas' celebrated adventure stories, '*Monte Cristo* and *The Three Musketeers,* which I never managed to finish reading, so invincible was the boredom that overwhelmed me at this accumulation of unbelievable fantasies' ('En Lisant', 9 March 1882).[13] Perhaps this is why he never mentions Jules Verne, whose foundational exploration and science fiction novels enjoyed an immense success from the 1860s. It is odd that a writer whose own stories often depend on dramatic adventures, extreme experiences and the fantastic should be so indifferent to popular authors whose exoticism, narrative verve and imaginative appeal may strike us as similar to Maupassant's. In his view, this is because writers like Dumas *père* lack true artistry, 'that singular quality of mind which creates something eternal, that unforgettable colour, changing with artists but always recognizable, which is the artistic soul' ('Question littéraire', 18 March 1882).[14] For the same reasons, he derides Victor Cherbuliez, a Swiss author elected to the French Academy, whose insipid novels arouse an 'invincible somnolence' and at their best aim to 'charm the tender soul of women' ('M. Victor Cherbuliez', 1 May 1883).[15]

Unlike many great nineteenth-century novelists such as Balzac and Flaubert, Maupassant had no interest in reconstructing the past in historical fiction. All his stories and novels are firmly set during the nineteenth century. (His only attempt to evoke medieval France was the unpublished and 'detestable' juvenile verse drama *La Trahison de la comtesse de Rhune*.)[16] He praises Dickens for his sense of place, for creating characters who are as 'palpable as beings actually encountered, while driving to the point of excess the need for physical detail'. All these are key elements in a novel's atmosphere, essential in 'making one feel the environment in which beings move, making possible the book's life'. At the same time, the writer or narrator should not intrude into this fictional world by imposing a psychological or moralizing commentary on its inhabitants ('Romans', 26 April 1882).[17] In his correspondence with Edmond de Goncourt, Maupassant diplomatically praised the precision and concision of the older novelist's somewhat mannered style (usually known as *écriture artiste*), his skill in opening new horizons and illuminating things anew in a single word (23 March 1877 and 3 April 1878). He was less sympathetic to younger imitators of so-called artistic writing, suggesting for example that Francis Poictevin's convoluted style was quite unnecessary to express subtleties of thought and emotion ('Batailles de livres', 28 October 1883).

He acknowledges, however, that common readers have little understanding of literary artistry and such refinements ('Poètes', 7 September 1882). Indeed, they exist on a different plane from the serious writer, for the latter is by definition a (self-) reflexive, alienated being:

> Everything he sees, everything he experiences, everything he feels, his joys, his pleasures, his suffering, his despair, instantaneously become subjects of observation. He analyses endlessly despite everything, despite himself, hearts, faces, gestures and intonations. ('L'Homme de lettres', 6 November 1882)[18]

Twenty-first-century readers may well doubt the general validity of these exclusions. Surely some writers can behave spontaneously and subdue the urge to register all experience? Surely novels with intrusive narrators (among whom one could include those of Balzac, Dickens and Tolstoy and many of their predecessors) are not always inherently flawed? Surely imaginatively absorbing action novels may be as interesting as those that are stylistically challenging and observationally precise (and Dumas or Robert Louis Stevenson more readable and enduring writers than Goncourt or Henry James)? In other words, Maupassant is delineating his personal preferences in fictional writing, rather than a coherent, inclusive theory of fiction.

His tastes were largely shaped by Flaubert, about whose life and work the author wrote about most extensively. In a preface to Flaubert's letters to George Sand (1884), Maupassant summarizes his mentor's theory and practice of literature. The doctrine of authorial impersonality is justified by the assertion that the writer's own personality is irrelevant: 'he must be the mirror of facts, but a mirror which reproduces them while giving them that inexpressible reflection, that mysterious, almost divine quality which is art'. Since things and facts are illusory, 'only relations are true, that is the way in which we perceive objects.' Style itself is a quasi-transcendent mode of perception that goes beyond transient phenomena: 'a unique, absolute way of expressing a thing in all its colour and intensity'. Indeed, 'words have a soul. Most readers and writers only ask them to have a sense.'[19]

In the essay entitled 'Le Roman', which was published with his short novel *Pierre et Jean* (1888), these notions are reiterated and clarified. While pleading for eclecticism of tastes and conceding that novels that emphasize intrigue and plot are valid, Maupassant insists that serious modern novelists are not romantic entertainers but should offer a personal vision of everyday experience which obliges readers to grasp 'the deep and hidden sense of events'. Realism is not an objective transcription of reality, but an efficacious literary convention which uses key details and compositional skills to create the illusion of reality (in other words, plausibility of character and situation, temporal causality and so forth). Just as our perception of the world is determined subjectively and variably by the limits of our senses and temperament, so too 'great artists are those who impose their particular illusion on humanity.' Novels which reveal characters' psychology through their actions and behaviour seem to him more sincere and credible than those in which characters' motivations and thoughts are ponderously explained and analysed by an external narrator. All characters are really disguised versions of the author who creates them. Finally, he deplores the contorted syntax and obscure lexis of *écriture artiste*: to express subtleties of thought and emotion, simplicity and precision are required.[20]

Such high-flown, ambitious assertions clearly reveal Maupassant in a quite different light from the self-declared mercenary pessimist we have glimpsed in previous chapters. A later chapter will return to the philosophic sources and conceptions that underlie both his pessimism and this celebration of artistic genius. The remainder of this chapter will study how successful Maupassant actually is in fulfilling this aesthetically and ethically demanding programme in his own writing. In the first place, it is helpful to sample some characteristic examples from the six genres which he practised (verse, drama; journalism and stories; travel writing and novels), to consider their evolution, and finally to examine stylistic and technical features in some detail. A simple progression is already implied by this list of genres: from verse to prose, from short stories and essays to longer novels and autobiographical travelogues. Or perhaps more subtly: from prosaic verse to poeticized prose, from brief fiction and ephemeral journalism based on economy of means and impact to books demanding much greater creative investment (and therefore offering something more substantial and durable). The problem, however, is that Maupassant's weakest work comes at the beginning and end of his career: setting aside the unfinished novels, few would claim that novels like *Fort comme la mort* (1889) and *Notre cœur* (1890) match any of the works produced in the mid-1880s (and arguably they fail to obey the criteria for serious fiction outlined in the previous paragraph).

The fundamental weakness of Maupassant's plays and poems is that they too patently lack the artistic originality in form and vision to which the author aspired. But since they also show his extraordinary (or for Flaubert, deplorable[21]) facility and rehearse themes found in his fiction, they deserve at least brief attention. Many of the pieces in *Des Vers* are unremarkable romantic lyrics cast in conventional rhyme and metre (typically, the twelve-syllable alexandrine), whose trite dexterity is occasionally enlivened by black humour or provocative excess. Love and its entanglements are frequent topics. Thus in 'Une Conquête', the lover's conquest proves all too easy:

> Poète au coeur naïf il cherchait une perle ;
> Trouvant un bijou faux, il le prit et fit bien.
> J'approuve le bon sens de cet adage ancien :
> « Quand on n'a pas de grive, il faut manger un merle. »[22]

Literally translated, the naive poet sought a pearl but finding a false jewel, he did well to keep it; this confirms the good sense of the old adage that says, if you can't have a thrush, eat a blackbird. This poem is figuratively a precursor to one of Maupassant's most famous stories, 'La Parure' (1884, also known as 'The Necklace' in English), whose misguided protagonist causes her ruin by ignoring its pragmatic moral (aspiring beyond her means and failing to distinguish real and fake jewels, in a literal rather than metaphorical sense). The dietary habits incidentally revealed in the last line may strike today's Anglo-American readers unused to consuming small birds as unwholesomely French.

The collection was actually reprinted three times after its publication in April 1880. While recognizing the author's forcefulness, reviewers like Henry Roujon observed that Maupassant wrote 'verse at the margins of poetry, sensual and wordy, the verse of a classy prose writer' (implying that his superficial mastery of rhyme and metre actually betrays how constrained he was by this form).[23] In some cases, however, the prosaic effect is deliberate. Thus in 'Fin d'amour', a bored lover abandons his mistress (the first of innumerable variations on this theme in later works):

> Il se leva, roulant entre ses doigts distraits
> La mince cigarette, et, d'une voix lassée :
> « Non, c'est fini, dit-il, à quoi bon les regrets ? »

The sense of these banal gestures and utterance can be translated into straightforward prose: 'He got up, rolling a slender cigarette distractedly between his fingers, and said wearily: "No, it's over, what's the use of regrets?"' This does however involve eliding some poetic touches that delicately heighten the exchange (normalizing the adjectives *distraits* and *lassée* by turning them into adverbs, losing the rhyme of *distraits* with 'regrets', which suggests how insignificant this rupture is). Elsewhere, Maupassant is overtly satirical, deriding bourgeois vanity and philistinism in 'Propos des rues'. He records this exchange: '"By the bye, have you read that fellow Zola?"/ "What filth!!!"', before concluding, with true Flaubertian misanthropy, that the silence of cattle is preferable to the garrulous stupidity of humans.

The most adventurous poems in the collection attempt to deal more frankly with sexuality. 'Au Bord de l'eau' (on its initial publication in a review, originally threatened with prosecution) is a lengthy narrative that coyly recounts the consummation of a riverside *Liebestod*:

> Ainsi que deux forçats rivés aux mêmes fers,
> Un lien nous tenait, l'affinité des chairs.

> (Like convicts whom the chain gang joins,
> We were bonded by our burning loins.)

Another long narrative, 'Vénus rustique', extends this theme of pantheistic eroticism into the realm of myth, of what subsists of antique gods or goddesses in modernity. Louis Forestier observes that such 'violently sensual naturalism' also anticipates Maupassant's later prose texts (such as those that celebrate erotic encounters in Mediterranean climes), and that *Des Vers* attempts to 'delineate and occupy a new poetic domain', the poetry of everyday realism, following his contemporary Jean Richepin's manifesto in *La Chanson des gueux* (1876) on behalf of free poetic expression (this anthology, *The Song of the Beggars*, earned Richepin a brief prison sentence for obscenity, although he was elected to the Académie française thirty years later).[24] Unsurprisingly, perhaps, Maupassant's explicitly obscene poems have an uninhibited comic verve not found in his polite public offerings; regrettably, although published clandestinely in Brussels and then posthumously, these bawdy pieces have never appeared in standard editions of his complete works. As titles like 'Minette', 'Ma Source' and '69' suggest, these celebrate the joys of oral-genital coupling with burlesque relish, or the androgynous delight of being mounted by 'La Femme à barbe'.[25]

Such pornographic exhibitionism provides an obvious link to Maupassant's first play, *A La feuille de rose, maison turque*, the burlesque farce performed privately by the author and male friends in 1875 and 1877. It was published in 1926 long after his death and never acknowledged in his complete works. Probably the writer, as he gained respectability, shared Marie-Claire Bancquart's later judgement that this brief sketch 'is not worth much and has lost all its scandalous savour'.[26] The Turkish house in the title is a euphemism for a brothel, and the rose leaf *fin-de-siècle* slang for anilingus. A well-endowed provincial mayor from Conville and his wife mistake the establishment for a hotel, and encounter a variety of sleazy characters such as a former seminarian employed to wash condoms, a hunchback, a stammering septic tank cleaner, a luscious (female) prostitute played by Maupassant, and a procurer who has his father's stuffed penis on display. The seminarian is nicknamed Crête-de-coq (meaning coxcomb or unsightly lesions caused by venereal disease), one of many awful puns. The play concludes its juvenile breaking of taboos with a bacchanal around the phallus. And yet for twenty-first-century readers, its uninspiring obscenity is probably less offensive than the way in which it unwittingly reinforces misogynist stereotypes. The fact that all parts were played by men (adorned with fake genitals) leads one feminist critic to conclude that women are excluded both as actors and readers by this indulgence of male (and homo-erotic) fantasies.[27] It is hard to believe that six years later the same author produced 'La Maison Tellier', an endearing story also set in a bordello, where the gross, puerile bawdry of this early farce is replaced by a provocative but moving defence of an institution shown to play an important role in the cultural and sexual life of a provincial community.

The immaturity and banality of Maupassant's early verse and plays, compared to stories and novels that treat similar topics and themes far less crudely, are due as much to his unease with the formal and generic problems posed by poetry and drama as to wider inexperience. Without the narratorial voice that allows him to create the atmosphere so essential for fiction or indeed travelogues (establishing for example people, places and relationships in skilfully modulated descriptive passages), Maupassant's writing seems strangely impoverished. Rather like the rustic lovers trapped by the affinity of the flesh (which he describes more coarsely in a letter about this poem), one feels Maupassant the would-be poet is equally shackled by the demands of rhyme and metre, which often drain all the colour and vigour from his language. This is particularly noticeable in the verse plays. He completed six plays (*Histoire du vieux temps, A La feuille de rose . . ., La Trahison de la comtesse de Rhune, Une Répétition, La Paix du ménage, Musotte*), leaving two or three others unfinished (*La Demande, Yvette*; and possibly *Mme Thomassin*, though he denied authorship). Three plays written in the 1870s are in verse: the sketches *Une Répétition* and *Histoire du vieux temps*, and the three-act tragic drama *La Trahison de la comtesse de Rhune*. Only *Histoire du vieux temps* was performed and published in the author's lifetime (it ran quite successfully in two theatres in early 1879).

Maupassant himself called these light sketches his 'acné mussétiste', a backhanded homage to the charming romantic plays composed by the poet Alfred de Musset in the 1830s. In *Histoire du vieux temps*, two ageing aristocrats in a Louis xv boudoir regret the winter of old age and a failed amorous flirtation in their youth. Both characters and their dialogue are unmemorable imitations of bygone writers as well as bygone times (unlike *A La feuille de rose*, which does at least represent taboo areas of modernity, in line with Maupassant's aesthetic programme). *Une Répétition* presents another perennial topic, the putative *ménage à trois* of elderly husband, young wife and aspiring younger lover. By rehearsing a Louis xv *bergerie* (pastoral piece), the wife and her swain are able to pursue their flirtation in front of the husband while impressing him with their acting skills. Such archaic, mannered posturing has little dramatic potential, although it introduces Maupassant's thesis that desirable women are easily able to manipulate and dominate men in the private sphere.

La Trahison de la comtesse de Rhune is Maupassant's most ambitious (and unperformable) play, although he soon recognized these ambitions had foundered, as already noted. Here he moves beyond the domestic sphere of wealthy idlers to evoke the powerful conflicted figures who drive the destiny of nations, as portrayed in the stirring historical dramas of Victor Hugo, Kleist, Schiller or indeed Shakespeare. The play is set in fourteenth-century Brittany, in a castle besieged by the English. The countess is a fatal beauty who betrays her nation, husband and a besotted page in favour of her English lover; but after all her plots are thwarted, she stabs herself, her lover is captured and drowned, and the naive pageboy is spared. Apart from the practical problems of staging a play by an unknown writer, with a large cast and elaborate set, the historical background is confusing, the action is rushed and melodramatic, the characters underdeveloped, the dialogue pedestrian and devoid of the poetic monologues and blending of sublime and grotesque one might expect from a pastiche of Hugo and Shakespeare. The author judged rightly that the whole enterprise was woefully misbegotten.

On the other hand, the plays written in prose and performed in the 1890s are much more workmanlike, probably because they are adaptations of previously published stories. *La Paix du ménage* was adapted in 1888 from the 1883 text 'Au Bord du lit', and after several revisions eventually performed in March 1893. Like a number of pieces published in story collections, the source text itself is actually a dramatic sketch, consisting entirely of dialogue between an estranged aristocratic couple, interspersed with brief stage directions (printed in italics, and shifting from the past to present tense after the introduction). The absence of a separate narrator means however that the dialogue has to transmit a lot of expository information (about the couple's deteriorating relationship, their lovers and so on), which renders much of it ponderously redundant and psychologically implausible. This objection applies equally to the staged version, which nevertheless in some ways improves on the original. For example, the aggressive rage behind the count's frustrated desire is compared to a rabid dog's urge to bite. In the original, as the title 'Au Bord du lit' implies, the wife demands payment for bedroom action if she is to be treated like a cocotte, and the count complies (as though cynically negotiating with a *professionnelle*). In the play, household peace at this price is unacceptable: the wife demands then haughtily rejects this demeaning monetary concession, and declares their relationship is finished. While confirming the wife's moral superiority, despite her husband's threatening antics, this change of ending does of course also tone down the insinuation that marriage is as much as prostitution a commercial relationship, which a bourgeois theatre audience would find unpalatable, if not unacceptable.

Musotte was Maupassant's most successful play, dramatically and financially. That it was co-authored with Jacques Normand is probably not coincidental, although it is impossible to disentangle how much each writer contributed. Normand was a prolific playwright and versifier, although his own work has long since sunk into oblivion. Here again, the source text was a story ('L'Enfant') first published in 1882. As the title suggests, the theme is the familiar one of illegitimate paternity. In six pages, we see how a worldly bachelor pays off his long-standing mistress in order to marry an innocent, respectable young woman. On his wedding night he learns however that this ex-mistress is dying after giving birth to his child. Stricken with guilt, he agrees to adopt the infant, and his new wife nobly welcomes what the narrator cannot resist calling 'the shrieking brat'.[28] The adaptation thus involved expanding and transforming this brief moral tale or parable of redemption and forgiveness (with its uncharacteristic happy ending and minimal characterization) into a three-act bourgeois drama with a fully realized cast, established settings, and extended plot. While the original story summarily depicts the chain of familial obligations linking the husband to the two women and baby, to sustain a two-hour play the authors were obliged not only to flesh out the principal characters, but to introduce a new set of secondary characters whose support or opposition allows for dramatic confrontations and earnest debates about the morality of illegitimacy and marriage. It is worth recalling that these were controversial issues: while divorce had been reintroduced in 1884, under the Napoleonic code of 1804, illegitimate children were still not legally recognized – that is, they had no entitlement to be supported by their 'natural' father. On the other hand, a husband was obliged to support a child born to his wife, even if he was not the biological father. Although protecting the bond of marriage, the law callously ignored the suffering and injustice thereby created. In nineteenth-century literature questions of personal and legal identity or filiation recur obsessively (as the innumerable deceived fathers and dispossessed children in Maupassant's works attest).[29]

Musotte (the name of the ex-mistress) is dedicated to Dumas *fils* (whose moralizing theatrical melodramas about fallen women Maupassant apparently respected more than his father's adventure yarns) and its pious sentimentality and consoling platitudes are unlikely to find much favour with twenty-first-century readers who associate *fin-de-siècle* European theatre with the radical dissonances of Ibsen, Strindberg or Jarry. But it was adroitly adapted to appeal to mainstream French audiences and critics who preferred uplifting and unchallenging drama (the very mendacious, conservative idealism which Maupassant himself had ostensibly rejected). On these undemanding terms (akin to modern TV and film adaptations which turn classic novels into hollowed-out costume dramas), the adaptation was a skilfully judged tearjerker. Among enthusiastic critics, Albert Wolff found the play 'exquisite and particularly touching' (*Le Figaro*, 5 March 1891).

If Maupassant's theatre is barely recognized nowadays, then, this is because it is either a bastardized version of his stories which falls short of the artistic ideals to which he aspired, or it is practically unperformable. But from a more pragmatic viewpoint, his better poems and plays still reveal an impressive professionalism, in terms of their relative critical and commercial success, even if his treatment of controversial themes is far more dexterous in prose fiction. Thus the priapic farce *A La feuille de rose* is arguably an obscene precursor of the bawdy comic sketches which enliven some story collections (usually involving

obtuse peasants in rural courtrooms). The crude mockery of a
Marseille accent in the play is also replaced in many stories by
more affectionate and accurate recording of Norman dialect. His
poetic impulses similarly found an outlet in the heightened style
which he evolved in his fiction and travel writing. The remainder
of this chapter will focus on generic and stylistic issues, and
more specifically on how Maupassant adapted the literary style
of late nineteenth-century French prose in his best writing, by
way of introduction to the discussion of his stories and novels in
succeeding chapters.

One characteristic of famous nineteenth-century realist novels
that strikes and perhaps overwhelms modern readers is their
immense length and density, compared to the sparer literary
fiction of the last century. Why do Balzac, Dickens and Dostoevsky
produce hundreds of pages, packing out their compelling central
themes and figures with interminable descriptions of every
setting, innumerable secondary characters, complex subplots,
and garrulous disquisitions on barely relevant sundry topics?
The novel becomes a totalizing enterprise: financially, more
lines of text mean more payment for serial rights; socially, the
novelist becomes an all-purpose commentator who precedes
the establishment of sociology as a discipline; aesthetically, the
novelist becomes a camera recording the material presence of
the external world that shapes the behaviour and subjectivity of
characters. In comparison, Maupassant is a minimalist, albeit
a prolific one: even his earlier novels are fairly short and they
become noticeably shorter. *Une Vie* occupies 192 pages; *Bel-Ami*,
283 pages; *Mont-Oriol*, 217 pages; *Pierre et Jean*, 116 pages; *Fort
comme la mort*, 191 pages; *Notre coeur*, 150 pages. Their total
combined length is considerably less than either Hugo's *Les
Misérables* or *Peace and War* (as Maupassant miscalled Tolstoy's
novel). While admiring Balzac's creative vitality, he found his

narrative style prolix and incoherent, comparing him to a man attempting to build a small house with material sufficient for a whole apartment block.

The short story in particular needs to match the economy of means and ends, especially when it is written to meet the demands of periodical publication. Henry James noted ruefully how well Maupassant achieved the necessary clarity, precision and concision, compared to his own digressive opacity.[30] Beyond his informative comments on longer fiction already discussed, Maupassant himself says almost nothing about the poetics of the *conte* and *nouvelle*, terms which he uses interchangeably. Such reticence and casualness are contrary to critical usage, which usually explicitly distinguishes the *nouvelle* as a longer story (sometimes verging on a novella or short novel), and reserves the term *conte* for tales that are more structurally or generically specific (such as folk, fairy, fantastic or philosophical tales). How far such conceptualizations and other taxonomies illuminate Maupassant's actual composition of particular types of stories will be discussed in the next chapter. It is more appropriate to conclude this chapter by examining his actual writing style, his engagement with language.

A good starting point is Edmond de Goncourt's patronizing dismissal. Complaining that Maupassant attacks him in the press while hypocritically flattering him in person, he adds:

> he may well be a very skilful storyteller from Normandy . . . but he is no writer, and he has his reasons for denigrating *artistic writing*. The [great] writer . . . signs his phrase and makes it recognizable to lettered readers, even without his signature . . . Now a page of Maupassant is not signed, it is quite simply good run-of-the mill copy that could belong to anybody.[31]

Goncourt's denigration is partly motivated by envious spite, but nonetheless this 1888 private diary entry has often been cited as a valid critique of Maupassant's literary deficiencies. Yet it rests on an assumption that is at best a matter of personal taste or just spurious: fiction writing that is difficult, that significantly deviates from ordinary usage (for example, by choice of unusual vocabulary, complex syntax or narrative spatio-temporal dislocation) is deemed to be inherently superior to a plainer, more readable style and plot line. In any case, more attentive and sympathetic reading of Maupassant soon reveals that his best writing is not mechanical hack-work but does in fact bear an authentic personal stamp. This is marked, for example, in innumerable succinct descriptive passages which engage his narrator and readers with places and landscapes.[32] Such descriptions are often notable for their evocative brevity, multi-sensual detail, and adroit functional integration into the narrative (unlike say, Balzac's long-winded inventories or Flaubert's over-elaborate discordant metaphors).

They also go beyond the conventionally picturesque. Contemplating the desert in *Au Soleil*: 'this calm, desolate landscape, streaming with light, is sufficient to the eye, is sufficient to thought, satisfies the senses and dreams, because it is complete, *absolute*, and could not be conceived differently.' At times, language seems inadequate to convey the intensity of the encounter: 'we leave at daybreak. The dawn is pink, an intense pink. How to express it?' For these are 'intangible colorations, so new for our organs accustomed to seeing the atmosphere of Europe' (*La Vie errante*). Maupassant's seascapes in *Sur l'eau* similarly go beyond technically brilliant evocation of marine phenomena (which Henri Mitterand compares favourably to Conrad),[33] to convey sublime terror at nature's awakening: 'the air is full of mysterious shiverings unknown to those still in their beds. One breathes, one drinks, one sees life reborn, the material life of the world, the life which courses through the stars, whose secret is our immense torment.'

This is patently 'artistic writing', even if less mannered than Goncourt's (which Maupassant actually never attacked). Goncourt

Edmond de Goncourt, photographed by Nadar in 1877.

refuses to recognize that they share similar aspirations and that Maupassant probably achieves his more effectively. Following Flaubert, both seek in their fiction to communicate the multi-dimensional subjectivity of individual experience in its interaction with external reality and the social world, while dispensing with explanatory narratorial commentary and melodramatic plotting. These shifts in narrative technique situate them at an interesting mid-point between the analytical objectivity of earlier realists and the solipsistic detachment from consensual reality and conventional storytelling of modernist writers like Proust. *L'écriture artiste* is a style adopted to facilitate this shifting mode of perception, which commentators like Marcel Cressot argue is better called literary impressionism,[34] since (like Monet's paintings) it attempts to seize phenomena in their immediacy, as they impinge on the observer's senses, detaching them from underlying relations of cause and effect. In practice, this involves considerable disruption to normal use of syntax and lexis: the removal of agents, personification of objects, using abstract nouns in place of adjectives, changing word order, using the durative aspect of verbs and present participles to stress states rather than actions, and so forth. Thus *regarder courir des blancheurs chevalines* foregrounds the blurred movement of white things, which the reader is obliged to resolve into 'watching white horses running', much as blobs of colour in a painting are eventually seen to represent identifiable beings and objects.

At its best, this achieves the poetically and psychologically innovative use of style which Maupassant sought to adopt from Flaubert; at its worst, it becomes the pretentious absurdity he derided in Poictevin. Jacques Dubois argues that while Flaubert and Maupassant practised a moderate, classical form of artistic writing (where overall narrative cohesion is retained), the Goncourt brothers and their lesser imitators follow a bolder project, which tends to degenerate into jargon, artifice or incontinence, as overwhelming descriptive detail freezes time and space and destroys dramatic unity.[35] André Vial's magisterial *Guy de Maupassant et l'art du roman* provides illuminating stylistic case studies, from which I will borrow some characteristic examples.

Vial likewise maintains that Maupassant reconciles classicism and literary impressionism: his lexis is simple and common, achieving rigour, elegance, expressivity and avoiding mannerism. Subtle shifts in usage, however, heighten the impact of a word or expression. He favours hypallage (marrying an epithet to an unexpected noun): thus 'the frozen silence of the fields'. He often uses key figures of *écriture artiste*, for example creating an exact, immediate impression with a metaphor in place of a more routine term: thus 'the round cheeks of the boats', 'his heart worm-eaten by love'. Or verbs are replaced by nouns, making characters the site of emotions rather than autonomous agents: thus 'to shiver with pleasure' becomes 'he gave a shiver of pleasure'.

Syntactically, sentences are organized to contrast duration and the instantaneous (the novel being a genre that primarily expresses duration, continuity and becoming). Present participles for example suggest progressive, continual action: 'The low sky, loaded with water, seemed to have burst, emptying on to the earth, reducing it to mush, melting it like sugar.' He favours asyndeton in paragraphs, avoiding subordinating conjunctions, because the novel is meant to be a vision, a continuous succession of images rather than a discourse or argument. Apposition is used to avoid subordination: 'an aristocrat by birth, he instinctively hated the Revolution.' His sentences have careful rhythms and cadences, although these sometimes become automatisms. Notable are generalizations beginning 'one of those . . . which/who', sometimes repeated in an enumeration; or ternary phrases, often crisply effective (*L'autre remercia, salua et disparut*, rather weakened in English: the other thanked him, saluted and disappeared). Vial observes more critically however that in weaker novels like

Self portrait by Émile Zola, taken shortly before his death in 1902.

Mont-Oriol and *Notre coeur*, the author's habitual verve, lucidity and satirical detachment tend to degenerate into somewhat hackneyed romantic phraseology and oratorical lyricism, serving up tired metaphors that are commonplaces of precious rhetoric (a character 'blows on the fire of his own heart').[36]

These last two chapters have deliberately offered a broad panorama of Maupassant's writing and the cultural context which allowed him to thrive in popular nineteenth-century genres probably unfamiliar to most modern readers (such as essayistic journalism and middlebrow drama), showing him as a commercially astute, all-round man of letters rather than simply an ingenious storyteller.

These closing paragraphs were likewise intended to suggest how culturally determined and important the more technical details of style and composition are, if we wish to appreciate his best writing (and explain why he sometimes fails to achieve his ambitions). In an 1880 essay on 'Personal Expression', Zola observed that writers lacking originality 'pick up the style which is in the air. They catch the phrases which fly around them', drawing on 'an immense store filled with well-known phrases and current expressions, a sort of average of stylistic usage'.[37] The same can be said of subject matter and compositional technique: here too originality involves skilfully judged deviation from accepted norms and conventions of propriety and presentation. Both Zola and Maupassant were determined to extend the boundaries of narrative fiction, without however sacrificing the popular appeal that made them rich and famous (and that evaded their unfortunate colleague Goncourt). How Maupassant's best-known work achieved these often conflicting ends is the subject of the following chapters.

4

Storyteller

Whereas the realistic social novel is largely an invention of the eighteenth and nineteenth centuries, the origins of the story are far more distant, long pre-dating the creation of writing systems and printing. About 70,000 years ago, the evolution of sophisticated language unknown in any other species allowed humans to attain the level of self-reflexivity and symbolic thought needed to generate storytelling. Subsequently, sacred myths of origins and secular folk tales, elaborated and transmitted orally for millennia, seem to have become universal characteristics of human societies. If we define stories as explanatory verbal narratives about human nature and behaviour, we should set aside the tacit assumption that their imaginary nature makes them trivial or redundant. As Jonathan Gottschall observes, 'we are, as a species, addicted to story. Even when the body goes to sleep, the mind stays up all night, telling itself stories.'[1] Humans' appetite for consuming endless stories in different media reinforces the argument that stories are central to both individual and collective social identity. The neurologist Oliver Sacks, for example, observes how patients suffering from memory loss in effect lose their life stories, the inner narrative whose continuous, unconscious construction establishes their unique self-awareness.[2] On a wider scale, the Israeli historian Yuval Noah Harari argues persuasively that the rise and success of complex human societies depended in large part on inventing shared collective narratives, purely imaginary belief systems that facilitate social cooperation and cohesion but have no grounding in the material, natural world. These range from religions, cultural traditions and political ideologies to corporations, money and other financial tools; they are so functionally integrated into human societies that it requires a conscious effort to recall that they were all made up by humans.[3]

These anthropological reflexions remind us that creating stories and fictional narratives had a primal function in the evolution of human culture that preceded the development of complex civilizations or written literature and its manifold sophisticated forms. We have already observed that Maupassant was a mediocre poet and playwright, a talented journalist, an innovative novelist and a brilliant storyteller. His fondness for presenting himself as a primitive, elemental being suggests his awareness of the fundamental impulses driving both his characters' behaviour and his own imagination. Indeed, one reason for his enduring and international appeal as a tale-teller, sometimes overlooked by commentators, is that many of his tales are rooted in the folkloric and mythic origins of the genre both structurally and thematically: note for example the frequency of embedded oral narration (that is, the presence of a character telling the story to other people) in the majority of his stories, or the innumerable variations on archetypal forms, conflict and cruelty, family rivalries and crises, and the vagaries of good or bad fortune, which are also staple themes of fairy tales. This is not to deny that Maupassant's stories are also firmly situated in a recognizable and accurately depicted social world, that of mid-nineteenth-century France. But notwithstanding the informative quality and precision of their material details (regarding customs, dialect, class, daily life and so forth), his stories retain an exotic allure, especially for modern readers for whom many of his characters and settings are as strangely unfamiliar as those in any traditional folk tale or its derivatives.

The vast expansion of literacy in mid-nineteenth-century France created a new reading public and growing market for accessible fiction that was mainly supplied by the popular daily press and more highbrow reviews. Although the novel was considered a more prestigious genre, nearly all the prose writers of the period also wrote short stories, if only because they could be produced more rapidly and published lucratively in a wide variety of periodicals. Whereas in the seventeenth and eighteenth century the *conte* is usually associated with a distinct type of exotic narrative, often conveying a moral or allegorical message (such as the fairy tales of Perrault and Madame d'Aulnoy or Voltaire's philosophical tales), the more realistic *nouvelle* is largely an invention of the nineteenth century, where the key reference points are Prosper Mérimée and Maupassant.[4] Mérimée's early short tales combine melodramatic plotlines, stylistic precision and picturesque detail with a fondness for the exotic and macabre. In characteristic stories like 'Tamango', 'L'Enlèvement de la redoute' and 'Mateo Falcone' (all published in 1829), he presents unsparing, horrific accounts of the slave trade, the Napoleonic wars and the barbaric code of honour that impels a Corsican to execute his young son for betraying a criminal to the authorities.

Writing fifty years later, Maupassant dispenses with Mérimée's romantic idealism and antiquarianism, but retains his quasi-ethnographic fascination with depicting cruelty and violence, sometimes tempered by an ironic detachment and black humour that derive more obviously from the fantastic tales of E.T.A. Hoffmann and Edgar Allan Poe. First translated into French respectively in 1828 and 1852, both these authors helped inspire the obsession with the grotesque, perverse and extremes of human experience characteristic not only of Maupassant but of many other of his contemporaries, such as Barbey d'Aurevilly, Huysmans, Octave Mirbeau and Jean Lorrain. That said, the most notable influence on Maupassant's technique as a storyteller (particularly his ability to evoke place and atmosphere and to depict the pathos of ordinary lives in a few telling details) was arguably Ivan Turgenev, whose accurate but unsentimental accounts of the harshness of Russian society in his stories and novels aroused so much hostility in his native country that he spent the last twelve years of his life in Paris (from where he acted as a useful ambassador, helping Maupassant and other French writers publish and promote their work in Russia). Turgenev however called his shorter pieces sketches rather than stories, and was followed by French writers who produced what are really collections of prose poems rather than narrative fiction (also following the example of Baudelaire's celebrated posthumous 1869 collection of *Petits poèmes en prose*). What distinguishes Maupassant from many contemporary writers of evocative short prose texts – such as Huysmans' *Croquis parisiens* (Parisian Sketches, 1880) – is his retention of the clear narrative arc of the story, the centrality of the plotline, and the resulting combination of concision and clarity, pathos and detachment, modernity and tradition that is probably his most significant contribution to the genre.

Maupassant published some three hundred stories in newspapers and reviews, which fill more than 2,600 pages in complete editions.[5] The majority are no longer than 3,000 words, their length determined in large part by the constraints of newspaper publication (that is, the need to maximize income through regular production, to meet pressing publication deadlines, and to fit within the space available in one issue). The relatively weaker stories usually betray creative fatigue, the author struggling to overcome these pressures by recycling old material and scenarios; we have already noted how Maupassant radically cut back his production of short texts from the mid-1880s. On the other hand, there are ten much longer stories which are all more than 8,000 words and among his best (several are discussed later in this chapter). In fact, Maupassant reissued only about 70 per cent of his stories in the fifteen volumes published during his lifetime; in other words, deliberately choosing to sacrifice nearly one hundred texts, which posthumous editors have resuscitated in innumerable combinations that sometimes bear no resemblance to the author's original intentions. For all his apparent carelessness and haste in reassembling stories in books (revealed in letters to publishers requesting they correct errors which breach contractual agreements), Maupassant's original anthologies do have an aesthetic and thematic coherence which later editions generally ignore or simply replace.[6]

In consequence, most readers probably sample only a small percentage of texts, often selected for anthologies by editors and translators who tend to avoid his more controversial topics (particularly in editions published before the 1960s). This has the unfortunate effect of greatly diminishing the reader's awareness of Maupassant's range and impact. Discussing this large corpus also raises some obvious practical and theoretical problems. Analysing a small number of outstanding stories in reasonable detail seems infinitely preferable to enumerating long lists of titles and favourite themes. However, before embarking on such an analysis, it is important to provide a broader overview, both of critical approaches and of the structural techniques that underpin many stories, since this will certainly enhance most readers' appreciation and understanding.

Early twentieth-century critics and editors of Maupassant's stories tended to approach them taxonomically via themes and subject matter. Thus in the 1930s René Dumesnil enumerated eight broad categories of tales, adding a ninth called 'miscellaneous subjects' to cover omissions.[7] Some modern publishers still follow this approach, with anthologies variously entitled *Contes parisiens*, *Contes cruels et fantastiques*, *Contes d'angoisse*, *Contes de la guerre* and so forth.[8] This has the advantage of conveying the breadth and diversity of topics covered in hundreds of stories; the drawback is that it says nothing about the significance of individual stories or the writer's literary skill. Perhaps the most thorough example of such cataloguing is provided by the Bouquins complete edition, which not only summarizes every story (in more than fifty pages) but also lists 79 themes over ten pages (though despite its apparent exhaustiveness, neither *guerre* (war) nor 'Paris' are listed). Nevertheless, such an index certainly reveals how threatening, dangerous and potentially tragic Maupassant's world is. Selecting three pages randomly, for example, one sees the headings 'debauch', 'devil', 'divorce', 'double', 'duel', 'strangling', 'fantastic', 'woman' (with the subheadings 'abandoned', 'dominating', 'unfaithful', 'seductress'), 'fire', 'madness', 'childbirth', 'impotence', 'incest', 'infanticide', 'infirmity' and 'drunkenness'.[9]

In the later twentieth century, commentators on Maupassant's works followed a welcome trend in literary criticism away from descriptive classification and biographical reductivism (the assumption that an author's writing is just a sort of coded expression of his personal life) to focus on the style, structure, impact and cultural significance of particular novels and stories. In other words, 'Boule de suif' is considered worth studying, not because Maupassant was personally involved in the Franco-Prussian war or possibly met a fat prostitute abused by German soldiers, but for its vivid account of the German invasion and the behaviour of French civilians, its skilful blend of satire, pathos and drama, and how it captures the reader's attention and interest in a variety of different ways.[10] Critics have also explored key narratological and generic features more carefully. These include how and by whom stories are narrated, how stories are constructed and plotted, as well as more ideological elements related to the author's world view and preconceptions, such as his presentation of gender and sexuality, social class and injustice, violence and insanity, his use of stereotypes and caricature.

An obvious starting point for any discussion of the story is its individual brevity (bearing in mind that famous medieval and early modern collections of interlinked stories by Chaucer, Boccaccio and Marguerite de Navarre actually run to hundreds of pages, and that Maupassant's stories collectively are more than twice as long as his six novels). Stories are neither better nor worse than longer works of prose fiction, but they are certainly quantitatively and qualitatively different. W. M. Landers offers a crisp summation of the tale's distinctiveness: 'Its law is economy, and all its components are brought to bear on a single focal point.'[11] Another commentator prefers the term 'revelatory situation'.[12] Personally, at least in Maupassant's case, I would replace focal point or revelation (which seem to imply a single event, perspective or transformative moment in time) with 'crisis or critical incident', since the crisis may trigger a succession of events (sometimes over a long period of time) and many people may be affected. Thus in 'La Parure', the true nature of the missing necklace is revealed only years after its disastrous loss; in 'Monsieur Parent', the eponymous cuckolded husband waits decades before finally confronting his adulterous wife and son and shattering their self-satisfied complacency.

While nineteenth-century novels in particular tend to be multi-dimensional, with multiple settings, characters, plotlines, discursive preambles and interventions by narrators, the successful story has a dramatic immediacy that is achieved by a ruthless narrowing of focus that recalls its primeval origins. As Robert Lethbridge puts it, 'unlike the novel as a genre, the short story retains an oral quality, its telling not that of a disembodied authorial voice but rather of a narrator regularly foregrounded, in Maupassant's case, by a double framing of teller and, thereby, embedded tale.'[13]

In some cases, such dramatic immediacy and efficacy are achieved by using first-person narrators (sometimes given additional plausibility by presenting themselves in diaries or letters, as in 'Le Horla') or by shifting from narration to dialogue, in order to give direct voice to characters (as in bawdy courtroom confrontations like 'Tribunaux rustiques'). More than 160 of Maupassant's stories are a 'transcript of an oral or occasionally a written narrative',[14] and about half of them have embedded narrators: that is, after a brief introduction, a character *within* the fictional setting intervenes to tell a tale to an audience in his (or occasionally her) own words. In many cases, the speaker's confidential, intense rapport with his listeners is an essential part of the narrative's effect; in 'Miss Harriet', for example, the audience is reduced to tears by the pitiful plight of the elderly spinster whom he describes.

There are other reasons for the frequent emphasis on narrative technique within stories. It effectively updates the embedded narrative sequences of much older European and Middle Eastern tale collections, such as *The Decameron* or *The 1,001 Nights* (which Maupassant obliquely references on a few occasions). E. D. Sullivan also suggests that the framed short tale 'was probably congenial to his vision of the world, which he tended to see in any case as fragmented, disjointed, partial, and lacking in fundamental connections'.[15] The framework also marks the point of entry into and return from experiences outside the competence and quotidian normality of most readers. More pragmatically, adopting a variety of narrators presented as fictional characters allows Maupassant as author not only to adopt a more detached or ironic perspective but plausibly to recount adventures and events far beyond his own experience. Whereas the geographical and social settings of his novels were all based on personal knowledge (of the Norman bourgeoisie and gentry, Parisian press, spa towns, and so on), we know almost nothing about the initial sources of his stories, other than that most of them must have been anecdotal or at second hand (derived from friends and acquaintances, newspaper reports or chance encounters).

Maupassant extends the nineteenth-century literary story by giving voice to narrators and graphically presenting characters and experiences usually marginalized or excluded from previous literary representation (such as madmen, murderers, prostitutes and peasants, or the sexual and violent abuse of women, children and animals). A small number of stories (which rarely feature in anthologies) still retain their shock effect, since they explicitly challenge sexual taboos about incest, child rape and abortion (for example, 'Monsieur Jocaste', 'Le Port', 'Châli', 'La Petite Roque', 'L'Enfant'). The classic story is also reinvigorated structurally, although in no sense does he seek to subvert plot-driven narrative, unlike his contemporaries Chekhov or the symbolist aesthete Villiers de l'Isle Adam (whose ironic macabre fantasies and whimsy in *Contes cruels* (1883) are likely to seem impenetrably obscure to many twenty-first-century readers).[16] Even when they deal with the fantastic or delusions, Maupassant's stories are invariably situated in a clearly delineated spatio-temporal reality and describe the effect of a linear sequence of events on characters whose physical and psychological traits are deftly sketched in. In many cases, characters are overwhelmed or radically affected by the events that befall them, usually with negative consequences (occasionally, they gain unexpected benefits).

Maupassant manipulates his characters (and readers) skilfully, in that the outcome of a story may overthrow their expectations, while remaining entirely plausible (as rereading will confirm). Critics have always stressed his use of the unexpected and surprise endings (not always with approval), what André Vial calls 'the final whip crack', with 'La Parure' being taken as paradigmatic.[17] In an interesting study of Maupassant's reception in the USA, Richard Fusco shows how his supposed mastery of the slick tale (popularized by mediocre translations) led in the 1890s to innumerable crude (but lucrative) imitations and to scornful rejection by more highbrow writers. Fusco also notes that

Maupassant's plot structure depends on rather more than an unexpected final reversal; as he points out, there are key turning points at various stages and different narrative configurations, often producing not so much a radical shift in events as a sudden moment of understanding for the central character.[18] Bernard Haezewindt argues very persuasively that Maupassant's texts demand both a primary, denotative reading (where the reader is absorbed in the flow of the narrative) and then a second, connotative reading (that is, a more analytic study, which reveals how a dense semantic network of minor descriptive details underpins the plot and determines our reactions).[19]

By way of transition to a fuller discussion of some of Maupassant's most impressive stories, it is useful to offer a few more specific illustrations of some of the critical points made in the preceding paragraphs. Some of his most characteristic features only become apparent if one systematically reads the whole corpus. Many are present throughout, whereas others are more intermittent. For example, an early tale like 'Sur l'eau' (1881) combines a lyrical appreciation of natural beauty (the moonlit fog lifts to reveal 'the river blazing with fire between two white mountains') with a sinister landscape that intensifies the narrator's morbid sense of dispossession ('there was within me something other than my will, and this other thing was afraid').[20] Such affinities and mood shifts recur throughout his work (as do intense visual images of fog, snow, moonlight and sunsets that match characters' feelings). Other early stories, however, are considerably less bleak than later stories which revisit similar scenarios. The war story 'Le Mariage du lieutenant Laré' (1878) was rewritten twice, the later versions becoming ever more complex and more pessimistic. Louis Forestier observes that 'in his early years Maupassant conforms to the public's taste for happy, not to say romantic, conclusions'.[21] But the ultimate gratification of characters' wishes also corresponds to the typical configuration of a fairy story: in 'Le Donneur d'eau bénite' (1877), an old couple finally rediscover their kidnapped son, the narrator observing sententiously 'they had worn down the tenacity of misfortune, for they were happy until they died'.[22] In 'Le Papa de Simon' (1879), an illegitimate peasant boy tormented by his schoolmates persuades the local blacksmith to become his stepfather by marrying his shamed mother, just as in 'Histoire d'une fille de ferme' (1881) a farmer agrees to marry his servant and adopt her child. Later, bastards and their parents are rarely so fortunate; misfortune and dissonance retain their tenacity.

Tolstoy would have approved of these harmonious solutions to sympathetic characters' dilemmas in these early stories, since he objected to Maupassant's cynicism, which he alleged showed a lack of moral sense (citing for instance his evident sympathy for the seducers in 'Une Partie de campagne'). He disliked the fact that Maupassant usually depicts the popular masses (typically, uneducated peasants rather than urban workers) as 'a horde of semi-brutes, moved only by sensuality, animosity and cupidity'.[23] But avarice does not necessarily preclude patriotic heroism, as Maupassant shows in certain war stories like 'La Mère Sauvage' and 'Saint-Antoine'. Maupassant refuses to sentimentalize human nature or deny the oppressive nature of social forces: the weak are often crushed or savagely abused, particularly when they are infirm, children or domestic animals (see 'L'Aveugle', 'Châli' or 'Histoire d'un chien'). Maupassant also delights in exposing the double standards of conventional sexual morality (which Tolstoy flouted shamelessly, for all his pious humanitarianism), often with mordant humour. In 'Ce cochon de Morin', the worldly politician Labarbe recounts how, in his younger days as a local journalist, he was asked to save a provincial shopkeeper from prosecution for embracing an attractive woman on the train. Labarbe succeeds beyond his expectations, since he not only pacifies the outraged lady's family but seduces the winsome victim. While Labarbe recalls their encounter with two homely erotic metaphors (reading the book of love until their candles burned down, and running his lips over her delicious cup of chocolate), the disgraced 'swine' Morin becomes a figure of ridicule and dies prematurely.[24] In other words, the real victim of the affair is the alleged assailant, who lacks the charm and enterprise needed to attain a goal which Maupassant regards as entirely desirable.

Sartre criticized Maupassant, not for subverting bourgeois sexual morality, but for his social elitism and complacency: in his view, a story like 'Ce cochon de Morin' may briefly disrupt conventional behaviour, but its resolution restores the order and privileges of the dominant class (from which Morin is excluded). Sartre complains that a typical Maupassant story involves self-satisfied males recounting a misadventure to an audience of their peers, which leaves them largely unscathed. He does not however discuss particular stories and seems unaware that many stories radically change or destroy their protagonists' previously placid existence.[25] Suicide is a frequent theme or outcome (as in 'Le Horla' or 'Promenade'); philandering males gloating over their conquests are humiliated or emasculated by women whose desirability and dominant personality give them almost supernatural power (as in 'L'Inconnue' and 'L'Inutile beauté').

While these illustrative remarks show something of Maupassant's impressive diversity, which is often underestimated even by prestigious commentators, his richest stories merit more detailed discussion. Inevitably, length is a determining factor in the texts selected. A story that is only a few pages long can do little more than sketch in a particular character, incident or encounter, sometimes arrestingly or movingly (as in bleak stories about callous mistreatment of the disabled and animals like 'L'Aveugle' or 'Pierrot'), sometimes crassly (as in 'La Toux', a hackneyed exercise in scatological humour, where coughing in bed is a puerile euphemism for breaking wind). Hence the writer's dissatisfaction with such frivolous *historiettes* and urge to concentrate on more substantial pieces, since a novella extending to twenty pages or more evidently gives him scope for developing exemplary characters, settings and incidents in far more depth and detail. Shorter tales could be also be improved by being integrated into novels or reworked as novellas. For example, Maupassant's two longest novellas are 'L'Héritage' (66 pages) and 'Yvette' (74 pages), much expanded revisions of 'Un Million' (five pages) and 'Yveline Samoris' (four pages).

'Boule de suif' is Maupassant's most celebrated novella. It merits further discussion essentially because it displays literary skills that raise him from a craftsman adroitly recounting the local and particular (comparable to Mérimée or O. Henry) to a tragicomic fabulist akin to Tolstoy, Chekhov or Kafka. It was written in 1879 and effectively launched his career when it was published in April 1880 in *Les Soirées de Médan*, an anthology of otherwise unremarkable stories by Zola and five associates, which marked the tenth anniversary of the Franco-Prussian war and affronted establishment critics with its unflattering depiction of the humiliating defeat and occupation that rapidly followed. 'Boule de suif', as Louis Forestier rightly observes, citing Flaubert, is 'a masterpiece of composition, comedy and observation'.[26] However, sympathetic readers will on first encounter more probably be moved by the patriotic prostitute's dilemma and final humiliation (to feel sympathy with the heroine and anger towards her spineless and hypocritical compatriots). Careful rereading will reveal in its forty pages (13,000 words) a further wealth of nuance, subtle detail and interpretive possibilities that significantly modify and extend this initial engagement in the dramatic confrontation of vanquished and victors. For example, the narrator also draws attention to Boule de suif's less admirable qualities and takes pains to develop the secondary characters who surround her beyond schematic caricatures of self-serving duplicity. Mockery of these characters' quirks or self-deception does not preclude awareness of their positive qualities. The social setting and material 'atmosphere' which Maupassant considered vital elements in bringing fictional people to life are also described with meticulous, sensual skill. On a symbolic level, the story can be read as a parable about warfare between nations and classes, or about collaboration and resistance (with evident parallels to the defeat and occupation in 1940 that make it an anticipatory model for innumerable twentieth-century narratives in fiction and film about Second World War France).

The story is set in Normandy, shortly after the city of Rouen was surrendered without any effective resistance and occupied by the German army on 6 December 1870. The circumstances of this local debacle are described in a preamble that fills as much space as the total length of Maupassant's shorter stories (in fact Boule de suif does not emerge as the central figure until the ninth page). This no doubt reflects Maupassant's personal involvement in the campaign and the overarching aim of *Les Soirées de Médan* to revisit this military and political catastrophe. But the main purpose is not to evoke the strategic and tactical blunders of politicians and generals, but rather to depict the impact of warfare on ordinary individuals and different social groups. First we are shown hordes of defeated and exhausted soldiers retreating through the city. Sympathy for individual suffering and patriotic dismay are rapidly replaced by a satirical account of the failings and pretensions of various military units and privileged groups. They resemble bandits rather than disciplined soldiers; their officers are self-important, incompetent poltroons; a few determined individuals surreptitiously murder German soldiers, but most of the inhabitants of Rouen are eager to placate their invaders and return to normality.

A small group of three influential businessmen and their wives obtain permission from the German authorities to travel to Le Havre (which remained unoccupied until the armistice signed on 28 January 1871). This tortuous journey involves travelling by stagecoach through occupied (that is, pacified) territory to Dieppe and then taking a ship. These six people represent commercial interests and social elites: the unscrupulous, affable wine merchant Loiseau and his shrewish spouse; and from 'a higher caste', the industrialist and local councillor M. Carré-Lamadon, and the wealthy landowner and politician comte Hubert de Bréville. As the narrator sarcastically remarks, these are 'honest, respectable people who have Religion and Principles'.[27] Four other voyagers join them: two taciturn devout nuns, and two rather more disreputable characters. These are Cornudet, an amiable revolutionary whose political activism largely amounts to speechifying and quaffing beer in republican cafés, and the chubby prostitute Élisabeth Rousset, who is nearly always referred to by the nickname 'Boule de suif'. This sobriquet could be translated more or less idiomatically as 'ball of suet', 'dumpling' or 'tub of lard', but is usually left in French, where it sounds less demeaning; in fact her attractive plumpness is presented as part of her sensual charm and comestibility (her face is like a red apple and her fingers like little sausages).

She is generous and patriotic, but also conscious of her status as a social outcast. Thus she deferentially shares her basket of provisions with the rest of the party, because this allows her to overcome their attempts to ostracize her (and the ladies share their foot-warmers with her and the nuns). But if social barriers are temporarily broken down by the demands of cold and hunger, her generosity and desire to please actually make her more vulnerable to subsequent events. Boule de suif reveals that she has fled Rouen after attacking a German soldier and is a fervent Bonapartist (thereby dissociating herself from her potential ally Cornudet, whose advances she also rejects). The narrator wryly notes that all women like assertive males and despotic governments (leaving the reader to recall that the debacle which destroyed the French Second Empire was actually the direct consequence of Napoleon III's

Prussian soldiers imposing the curfew on an occupied French town, attributed to Frédéric Lix and Amédée Daudenarde, 1873.

military and political ineptitude).[28] After being delayed by heavy snowfall, the coach is further detained in Tôtes, when the travellers are held hostage by the German commandant who wishes to enjoy Boule de suif's favours. Despite their expressions of indignation, after three days the rest of the group finally persuade her to accede to this demand (with the exception of Cornudet who denounces their complicity). When they finally depart, her humiliation and rejection are intensified when the others enjoy a hearty picnic from which she is excluded; as the anguished Boule de suif weeps, Cornudet sarcastically whistles *La Marseillaise*.

As this outline suggests, the story is constructed around a series of ironic contrasts that help engage the reader in the dramatic unfolding of resistance, collaboration and rejection, and also communicate Maupassant's unsentimental views of human behaviour and group dynamics. Some contrasts are fairly direct and perhaps unduly underscored by the narrator: thus Boule de suif's generosity (in sharing her food and body) is

'Master and servant', 1871. Caricature by Faustin Betbeder showing Napoleon III dressed as a monk and General Louis Jules Trochu dressed as a member of the clergy, tied to a post labelled 'L'homme de Sedan. L'homme de Paris'. Both men were held responsible for the French defeat which ended the Franco-Prussian War.

ACTUALITE PAR FAUSTIN

MAITRE ET VALET

contrasted with the self-centred and hypocritical meanness of the wealthier members of the group in the final scene. While neither the 'democrat' Cornudet nor the nuns offer her any consolation, the narrator conveys her frustrated rage at 'these honest rogues who had first sacrificed then rejected her, like something defiled and useless'.[29] The meaning of Cornudet's whistling (somewhat improbably counterpointed for hours with Boule de suif's sobbing) is less apparent. Twenty-first-century readers may recall that the words of Rouget de Lisle's 1792 revolutionary anthem *La Marseillaise* call for solidarity and resistance against tyrannical Germanic invaders, whereas we have just witnessed a group of upright citizens betray their most vulnerable compatriot to German lusts. In fact, *La Marseillaise* was restored as the national anthem only in 1879, when the Third Republic was securely established, and rapidly became the ritualized expression of the self-serving social conformism which Maupassant derided. In 1870, then, whistling the song is either anachronistic,[30] or simply another example of Cornudet's revolutionary posturing (he enjoys baiting his political adversaries, while doing nothing to aid or comfort the victim of their exploitation).

Although secondary characters are presented in a schematic or stereotyped way, in line with Maupassant's generally satirical attitude towards their behaviour (Cornudet's beer-drinking and beard-pulling, the inn-keeper's asthmatic wheezing, the nuns' obsessive devotions, the arrogant brutality of the dandyish German officer), at times they are invested with unexpected qualities. Thus Mme Follenvie (the inn-keeper's wife) suddenly delivers an impassioned and persuasive denunciation of warfare.[31] The pockmarked older nun emerges from her habitual silence to justify the merits of self-sacrifice for a higher cause, which further saps Boule de suif's resistance; she also reveals that she and her companion are nurses whose mission in Le Havre is to care for hundreds of soldiers suffering from smallpox (a disease which she herself has presumably survived). Despite their unsophisticated religious fanaticism, the nuns' genuine dedication to serving others subverts Boule de suif's scruples and implies that the prostitute's defiant pride, much like Cornudet's radicalism, is little more than self-deceiving posturing (just as she decides to attend a christening although she has abandoned her own child with foster parents).

Many other telling descriptive details could be cited that demonstrate how Maupassant adds material and symbolic depth to the story's setting as well as its characters. As the travellers finally depart, for example, the winter sun shines dazzlingly on the snow, while an army of white pigeons pick at the dung lying between the horses' legs; the storm has passed, the crisis is resolved, but the joyful purity of the scene is deliberately spoiled by the birds scrabbling in excrement. No doubt Boule de suif will survive her humiliation; what has been lost is the original sense of patriotism, altruism and solidarity which she stimulated in her companions. Just as the French army becomes an undisciplined rabble when confronted with German might, so too representatives of the national community display the basest egotism and craven connivance. When Maupassant returned to the war in later stories, he was reluctant to repeat such a caustic condemnation. In 'Mademoiselle Fifi' and 'Un Duel', for example, intimidating German officers are somewhat implausibly killed by civilians whom they attempt to humiliate, as though the author wished to seek redress for showing collaboration rather than revenge as the characteristic French response in 'Boule de suif'.

Although it is significantly different from extended novellas like 'Boule de suif', 'La Parure' is also one of Maupassant's most celebrated shorter stories, mainly because of the author's technical skill in reversing the premise of an earlier story called 'Les Bijoux' (1883). Readers and critics who dislike 'La Parure' might therefore add to their objections that it is a much imitated story about fake jewels that is itself an imitation of a story about genuine jewels. Francis Steegmuller complains that 'La Parure' makes the ordinary reader 'feel bad', and compares its shock ending to the sadistic practical jokes which Maupassant enjoyed; he adds that it gives a false impression of his work, since 'character, atmosphere, sentiment, and subtle comment on human life' are overridden by the contrived plot.[32] Yet, within the constraints of a 3,000-word tale, a more sympathetic reading will find all these qualities.

'La Parure' is usually translated into English as 'The Necklace', although this considerably narrows the sense of *parure*, which primarily means display and adornment. In 'Les Bijoux', a civil servant's charming wife feels *le besoin de se parer* (the urge to adorn herself), which she gratifies by acquiring a collection of false jewels.[33] After her sudden death, however, the bereaved husband discovers that the bling is the real thing. To his astonishment, the collection is worth a fortune (200,000 francs); his spouse had a secret life as a high-class courtesan servicing wealthy admirers. This unexpected windfall allows him to abandon work and live for pleasure, until he marries a virtuous harridan who makes his existence a misery. Bad fortune follows good fortune twice, as the ingenuous protagonist misjudges the temperament and potential for happiness of both his wives.

By delaying and reversing the revelation, and developing the central characters, 'La Parure' turns a comic sketch into a minor tragedy. An attractive young woman who aspires to a life of luxury and romance is obliged to marry a modest clerk in the Ministry of Instruction. Her dreams are briefly fulfilled when they are invited to the minister's ball; but on the way home she loses the magnificent diamond necklace lent to her by a wealthy friend. After ten years of drudgery, they pay back the cost of a replacement, only to discover that the original necklace was worth a fraction of the immense debt they needlessly contracted. This outline does not really do justice to a story whose intricacies and implications invite interpretation and analysis structurally, psychologically and morally. We might ask, for example, whether the ending seems contrived or follows a coherent necessity; whether the characters' behaviour is plausible; whether they engineer their own downfall or are victims of fate (or the author's malevolence).

Structurally, 'La Parure' recycles and reverses a plot device not only from an earlier Maupassant story, but does the same generically with the folkloric Cinderella motif, since it is an anti-fairytale: displaying her borrowed finery at the ball, before rushing away in a shabby cab and dropping the necklace, leads to the heroine's ruin, condemning her to a life of unrewarding toil. (Jewels are often a symbol of danger as much as glamorous wealth in fiction: retrieving lost jewels is thus a frequent device in adventure stories, such as Dumas' *Three Musketeers* and Wilkie Collins's *The Moonstone*.)

Prussian soldiers execute the heroine of 'La Mère Sauvage': illustration by Charles Morel for an edition of 1901.

As Bernard Haezewindt argues, the story has an internal logic that makes the crushing conclusion seem appropriate rather than arbitrary.[34] The 'proud and naive' Mathilde Loisel learns that the diamonds were false, their value illusory, as were her dreams, friendship with Mme Forestier, and the debt which Mathilde and her husband erroneously assumed they owed. While Robert Lethbridge suggests optimistically that the couple at least show 'a fundamental honesty not vitiated by their precarious financial circumstances', this overlooks the fact that concealment and vanity are the main cause of their downfall.[35] Had they admitted the loss of the jewels to Mme Forestier, they would have discovered their modest value (and understood her willingness to lend them to someone not a social equal). The consoling thought that the Loisels are entitled to reclaim the genuine necklace they have paid for is not entertained in the text, and dismissed by Haezewindt as a 'superficial reading';[36] perhaps it invites a further retelling in another sequel.

The opening sentence of 'La Parure' tells us that 'she was one of those pretty, charming girls born, as though by an error of destiny, into a family of clerks.'[37] The characteristic generalizing turn of phrase *une de ces*, however, firmly situates her within a social category (trapped in 'her caste', as the narrator writes) which Haezewindt argues is too commonplace for a tragic heroine.[38] Perhaps Maupassant democratizes tragedy; he certainly echoes the archetypal, much imitated French novel about a frustrated bourgeois wife whose romantic folly destroys herself and her family, Flaubert's *Madame Bovary* (1857). Mathilde's yearnings for luxury and adventure, and frustration with her drab household (ominously situated in the rue des Martyrs) and amiable, unambitious husband, are in fact calqued on almost identical passages in Flaubert's novel (Emma Bovary is overjoyed at being invited to an aristocratic ball, but thereafter this only intensifies her ennui and frustration). That Mathilde is a stereotypical sufferer from *bovarysme* makes the idle banality of her dreams even more apparent.

In fact, the Loisels enjoy a comfortable albeit modest existence which is overturned by Mathilde's self-indulgent extravagance and her husband's compliant support. Maupassant's relentless accounting for their expenditure makes this plain. Thus her husband lets her spend 400 francs on a dress (the equivalent of almost £5,000, with which he had planned to purchase a gun and fund hunting trips). Replacing the missing necklace costs 36,000 francs, half of which is paid for from savings (an indication of their relative prosperity), and the rest by borrowing. In ten years, they pay back a debt amounting to about £210,000, a remarkable achievement, which involves the devoted Loisel taking on three jobs concurrently. Mme Loisel herself is utterly transformed, morally and physically. She heroically accepts 'the horrible life of the needy', living in a garret and undertaking all the menial household tasks herself, in effect becoming a coarse working-class woman in behaviour and appearance.[39] Twenty-first-century readers (who survive without servants, and happily combine running their households with paid employment) may find this account of Mathilde's social demotion and physical degradation somewhat improbable, and conclude that the author's desire to make the story a parable overrides verisimilitude. But the physical demands of performing hard manual labour, and psychological shock of surviving in poverty in conditions far harsher than most of us endure, should not be underestimated.

Mme Loisel does indeed see herself as a victim of fate ('How little it takes to ruin or save you!'),[40] who has honourably paid back her large (but unacknowledged and imaginary) debt. Yet sacrificing herself to this unnecessary obligation was just another romantic illusion. Like many of Maupassant's characters, she unwittingly falls into a trap of her own making.[41] The lost necklace was actually worth 500 francs (a little more than the new dress). In other words, the false jewels were certainly not worthless (the party outfit costing in total 900 francs, or around

£11,000), still luxury goods for a modest household, but not ruinously unaffordable like the replacement which the couple rashly acquired. Haezewindt suggests that her failure to discern (or even to consider) the difference between the two necklaces shows she lacks the *savoir-vivre* required to move in high society, which includes recognizing and evaluating the adornments of luxury which its members display. Just as Boule de suif's ultimate humiliation is increased by her proudly confrontational rejection of the Prussian officer, so Mme Loisel's vainglorious display of finery and refusal to admit its loss seal her fate. Whereas her self-centred naivety is foolish rather than tragic, most readers will be moved by Boule de suif's capitulation and shabby treatment, because the prostitute's generous, altruistic nature is skilfully established and individualized. 'La Parure', on the other hand, concentrates primarily on the stereotyped characters' trajectory and entrapment rather than their personalities, offering a rather unedifying lesson about social pretensions and self-deception; neither husband nor wife possess the ruthless opportunism and pragmatism needed to rise above their mediocre situation (unlike the unscrupulous hero of *Bel-Ami*, whose initial circumstances are worse than theirs).

Like most of Maupassant's fiction, these stories show ordinary people confronting momentous personal crises in their everyday lives, often in desperate circumstances (warfare, poverty, illness, family breakdown). Despite their gravity, these circumstances do generally conform to the consensual social and psychological reality recognized by contemporary and later readers. Some of his most interesting stories, however, depict extreme experiences unknown to most readers and at times unknowable, in that they defy rational explanation and the laws of nature. Perhaps two or three dozen stories fit this category, depending on where the boundaries of normality and perception are set. From the outset,

Maupassant shows a fascination in his stories with the macabre and fantastic that recalls the phantasmagoria of Hoffmann and Poe: witness the appearance throughout the corpus of vengeful disembodied hands, sadistic killers and sinister corpses of people and animals, menacing doubles and spirits, inexplicable bouts of panic and terror, innumerable variations on insanity and alienation (see for example 'La Chevelure', 'Le Docteur Héraclius Gloss', 'Un Fou?', 'Magnétisme', 'La Main d'écorché', 'La Petite Roque', 'Qui sait?', 'Sur l'eau'). In many cases, a character's delusional or psychopathic behaviour is ultimately contained (if not explained), typically by sequestration in an asylum, imprisonment or suicide; normality is restored by his exclusion from everyday social life. Parallels with Maupassant's own fate are unavoidable, but it is a mistake to interpret the stories simply as symptoms of his mental decline: they have a coherence and lucidity remote from the uncontrolled ravings and seizures of syphilitic paresis, and derive from a long-standing literary and folkloric tradition.

In an essay on 'Le Fantastique' (1883), Maupassant asserted that scientific advances and rationalism had effectively eliminated the supernatural as an explanatory concept and that fantastic literature would consequently become obsolete. The prediction was wrong; in the following centuries, for all their technological progress and materialistic consumerism, fantasy films and literature have thrived, along with spiritualism and fundamentalist religions. But this argument does indicate how his approach to the terrors of the unknown differs from his predecessors: it is not based on external agents or transcendent worlds disrupting the material here and now, but rather on the dissolution of the self by mysterious forces that often emerge from within the body or psyche. Maupassant anticipates Freud's assertion that the supernatural is fabricated by the projection of internal mental disturbance on to external reality.[42] But the disturbance goes beyond illness. The most troubling stories depict the onset of extreme forms of alienation, where madness becomes a frightening but alluring gateway to perception, and is not necessarily delusional.

In 'Madame Hermet' (1887), the narrator states:

> The mad attract me. Such people live in a mysterious land of bizarre dreams, in an impenetrable cloud of insanity, where everything they have seen on earth, everything they have loved, everything they have done, begins anew for them in an imagined existence outside all the laws which govern things and control human thought.[43]

In 'La Peur' (1884), we are asked: 'who can tell who is sane and who is mad, in this life where reason should often be called folly and madness genius?'[44] In 'Un Fou?' (1884), Jacques Parent is driven mad by his hypnotic powers and magnetic hands, for 'it's like another being trapped within me, constantly trying to escape and act despite myself, stirring, gnawing and exhausting me.'[45] Marie-Claire Bancquart suggests that only two stories ('La Nuit' and 'Qui sait?') describe events which remain physically inexplicable (assuming one gives credence to the narrators' accounts, since no alternative interpretation is proposed).[46] As she says, Maupassant distorts the everyday but offers no objective possibility of the supernatural, unlike his renowned predecessors. His stories encapsulate the uncanny (as later theorized by Todorov), in that they attempt to rationalize the mysterious while demonstrating that it destroys rationality (whereas most fantastic stories admit the existence of a threshold to other worlds, dimensions and modes of being).[47]

These points are clarified and illustrated by discussing Maupassant's best-known exercise in the genre, 'Le Horla'. He produced two versions in 1886 and 1887, but only the second was published as the title piece of a story collection. It is however interesting to compare the draft and definitive versions, since the additions and omissions in the second sharpen and deepen the narrative (and show how recycling material invariably allowed the writer to improve his work both aesthetically and thematically). The first version is nine pages long and describes how a patient detained in a clinic presents his own case to a group of medical specialists, with the intention of proving his sanity. His comfortable, solitary existence in the Norman countryside has been disrupted by a sickness, which he attributes to a mysterious being that is draining his vitality, particularly during his sleep. The invisible being also consumes milk and water left in his bedroom overnight. His coachman and a neighbour suffer similar symptoms. Further signs of the creature's presence are reported: an invisible hand plucks a rose, opens doors and turns the pages of a book. Baptizing it 'Le Horla', he finally perceives the outline of its translucent body when it blocks his reflection in a full-length mirror. At this point, he takes refuge in the clinic to escape further attacks. The doctor confirms that three of his neighbours are now suffering similar symptoms; a newspaper reports that a province in Brazil has experienced the same epidemic. The doctor is unsure whether both he and his patient are mad, or have encountered a new race of beings destined to enslave humanity.

The revised version of 'Le Horla' is three times longer and presented as a diary written by an anonymous narrator. In other words, it dispenses with the objective narrative framing and external witnesses of the first draft, replacing what is a collective experience with the subjectivity of a tormented consciousness.[48] The diary covers four months (from May to September), which can be broken down into four distinct episodes that expand the account of his decline and illustrate the metaphysical musings that conclude the draft version. The central figure is also developed more as a personality (obsessive, curious, egotistical but pitiful). The opening entry records his *joie de vivre* and visceral attachment to the native region and property which shape his identity; among the ships passing along the Seine, he notes 'a superb Brazilian three-master'.[49] The following weeks mark his unaccountable mental and physical decline and sense of being possessed while asleep, until he resolves to escape elsewhere. After a month away, he returns claiming to be cured (2 July), and describes a trip to Mont Saint-Michel, where he discussed various supernatural phenomena with a monk that perhaps merely reveal the limitations of human senses and understanding. Within a day, however, his symptoms return, and he observes they are shared with his coachman. While insisting on (then doubting) his sanity, he speculates that, like a somnambulist, his mind may be occupied either by an unconscious, second self, or some outside being able to control his body. To escape his anguished torment, he retreats to Paris (12 July).

The third section describes the following eighteen days spent in Paris, where leading a more sociable existence removes the symptoms, for 'when we are alone for too long, we people the void with fantoms.'[50] While the rowdy celebrations on 14 July provoke misanthropic thoughts about people's servile acceptance of authority and illusory principles, watching a hypnotism session conducted by a doctor (which verges on the supernatural, since a visiting card is used as a mirror) confirms the existence of mysterious, inexplicable forces that allow the hypnotist to control another's will and awareness. Returning to Normandy in the final section, he becomes convinced that the Horla is a material being imperceptible to human senses which is gradually taking over his mind and driving his behaviour (while also wondering if its manifestations may be hallucinatory). Resolving to destroy it, he traps it in his bedroom and sets fire to his house, leaving his unfortunate servants to die in the blaze. Remaining unsure whether the Horla is physically destructible, he finally decides to kill himself.

The extended version of 'Le Horla' thus provides extra information that paradoxically increases the reader's uncertainty about how to interpret the story. While the doctor who basically confirms the narrator's account in the draft is omitted, the monk and hypnotist added to the final version may reinforce the narrator's convictions but leave the reader thinking him to be as deluded as was his hypnotized cousin. Richard Fusco argues that the novella establishes 'the irresolvable supernatural-insanity dichotomy that Poe had employed repeatedly': that is, either the narrator may be mad or the 'specter really exists'.[51] This however understates the narrative's more complex, dialectical evolution (from disbelief to partial belief and finally harrowing uncertainty). The narrator manifestly charts his own mental breakdown and solipsistic detachment from everyday reality and social bonds, demonstrated in its most extreme form in his final act of arson. Irrespective of whether the Horla exists outside his imagination or not, the narrator surely qualifies as psychotic by his own and any other judgement. But at the same time, the narrative convincingly supplies both specific evidence of the creature's existence and an empirical, epistemological framework that supports the possibility of its existence in the real world. Whatever else it may be, the Horla is certainly not a spectre (that is, a supernatural phantom returned from the realm of the dead). The narrator is ultimately driven mad by his inability to resist its dominating presence, made all the more fearsome by its intangibility.

While the narrator himself considers the possibility that the Horla is a hallucinatory phenomenon, the text deliberately provides evidence that suggests it actually exists, even if the nature of its existence remains highly problematic. For example, its objective presence in the house is attested by the inexplicable disappearance of milk and water and the illness of the coachman, even if we discount its fondness for roses and reading poetry as products of the narrator's imagination. Similarly, the newspaper report of a similar epidemic in Brazil lends credibility to the narrator's deduction that it arrived on the Brazilian ship. Whether the Horla is really a sentient being destined to subjugate humanity remains a speculative notion; the scene where it effaces the narrator's reflection in the mirror tells us more about his loss of selfhood than it does about the Horla's physical nature or intentions. But as most commentators note, the name Horla evokes something 'out there', an unknowable external agent that invades the mind and body of its victim, much like the imperceptible microbes that slowly sapped the vitality and lucidity of the author of the story.

Todorov observes that in Maupassant's stories, 'the supernatural provokes such anguish and horror that we are barely able to distinguish what constitutes it.'[52] In fact, Maupassant rejects the supernatural as an explanatory concept: we are confronted with something inexplicable that overwhelms and destroys the protagonist. Whatever its origins, the Horla is a malevolent double that dispossesses the narrator, inviting both literal and symbolic interpretations (as an alien invader, symptom and/or cause of insanity, unknown pathogen and so on). Doubling and dispossession recur frequently in his stories and novels, although usually in a more realistic context, typically that of family dramas involving parental, sibling or inter-generational conflict.

One powerful example is a less well-known later novella, 'Le Champ d'oliviers' (The Olive Grove, 1890). The central character is the abbé Vilbois, the local priest in a Provençal fishing village, whose troubled past is recalled in the opening pages. His uncharacteristic physical vigour and domineering presence are explained by his aristocratic, worldly origins and violent temperament. Twenty-five years earlier, after discovering his pregnant mistress had betrayed him, he was on the point of killing her, 'to annihilate this double shame', but was deterred only when she swore the child was not his.[53] Withdrawing from society, he took up holy orders. His placid existence is disturbed by the arrival of a sinister vagabond, an insolent young man, who claims to be the son born from this relationship. Their physical resemblance and the man's possession of his photograph convince the priest that the beggar is indeed his son.

In the course of an evening, the son reveals himself to be an abject villain. Rejected by his mother and stepfather, as an adolescent he was despatched to a reform school, which set him on the path of iniquity. His exploits include drowning a family in a drunken prank and, after the death of his mother, robbing and torturing his stepfather (whom he branded with a red-hot poker), for which sadistic crime he was imprisoned for three years. After the men quarrel violently, the priest's terrified housekeeper seeks help: the village authorities discover the priest with his throat cut and the son lying in a drunken stupor. The conclusion of the story initially serialized in *Le Figaro* then describes the son's arrest, trial, conviction and execution for murder, despite his pleas of innocence; the final version deletes this lengthy epilogue and ends with the laconic phrase 'the idea occurred to nobody that abbé Vilbois had perhaps taken his own life'.[54] Rather like the narrator of 'Le Horla', by sacrificing himself the priest ensures the elimination of his monstrous double, a loathsome parasite who embodies his parents' sinfulness and worst defects.

The grim misfortune which strikes the protagonists of the three stories discussed earlier, and so many others, is magnified in 'Le Champ d'oliviers' into a baleful, tragic destiny which drives penitent father and satanic son to mutual destruction. The olive grove which initially offered a peaceful refuge from past sins becomes a place of vengeance and redemption, however unorthodox (as a brief reference to its biblical connections and the priest's appeal to God imply). Shrouded in darkness, the lights carried by the search party reveal 'the tormented trunks of the olive trees sometimes resembling monsters, intertwined and twisted hellish serpents'.[55] But if the story remains gripping and memorable, it is less because of this melodramatic outcome

The long-awaited uncle returns in 'Mon oncle Jules': illustration by Morel (1901).

than through its gradual transformation of the idyllic milieu and unleashing of the characters' homicidal impulses.

Not all of Maupassant's stories conclude so bleakly, of course, although the more harmonious, comic idylls recounted in novellas like 'La Maison Tellier' and 'Les Soeurs Rondoli' are far less typical than the narratives of disruption discussed here. But characters in fiction whose lives are blighted are not real people; their tragic fates engage and affect us aesthetically, and Maupassant's achievement as a storyteller is primarily in the telling, the enticement of the reader's imagination through the dextrous evocation of setting, characters and dramatic conflict. In fact, his attempt to encapsulate Turgenev's originality as an author of stories reads like an aspiring self-portrait:

> A psychologist, physiologist and artist of the first rank, he is able in a few pages to create an absolute work, to link circumstances marvellously, to sketch living, palpable, arresting figures in a few strokes that are so light and skilful that one struggles to understand how so much depth is obtained with such apparently simple means. From each of his short stories there rises a vaporous melancholy, a deep sadness hidden under the bare facts (*Le Gaulois*, 21 November 1880).[56]

If brevity, minimalism and immediacy are the secret of success, it remains to consider how far Maupassant was able replicate these achievements in the longer and more discursive form of the novel.

5

Novelist

Maupassant published six novels between 1883 and 1890, leaving two more unfinished when he ceased writing in 1891. All of them were serialized in the press prior to book publication, reviewed sympathetically, and sold well during his lifetime. In this sense, he achieved both his commercial and aesthetic aspirations by producing ambitious works in a prestigious genre that established him with his contemporaries as something more than a writer of ephemeral stories and articles, a mere entertainer. Yet in the longer term, as regards his reputation with posterity, the immense effort which he invested in writing longer fiction has had rather mixed results: if two of his novels (*Bel-Ami* and *Pierre et Jean*) have continued to attract readers and critical appreciation, only the most devoted admirers read his other novels, apart perhaps from his debut work *Une Vie*. *Bel-Ami* is Maupassant's most substantial novel, not merely in terms of length but also in its range; it offers a dominant central character and broad social panorama that quite intentionally rival those of Balzac, Stendhal, Flaubert and Zola. On the other hand, *Pierre et Jean*, a claustrophobically intense study of family jealousy and rivalry, is by far his shortest novel: although it is only about twice the length of a novella like 'Yvette', Maupassant was insistent that its psychological depth still made it a *petit roman*.

That said, despite more obvious shortcomings, the four other novels have the readability, charm and lucidity that are so characteristic of the writer (and not infrequently lacking in nineteenth-century literary authors, which explains perhaps why some highbrow critics are blind to such qualities). Though often overlooked, *Mont-Oriol* is an engaging satirical account of adultery and financial speculation set in a provincial spa. While *Une Vie* rehearses the tragic failure of ambition, love and marriage established a generation earlier in Flaubert's *Madame Bovary*, the later works' exploration of psychological obsession anticipates twentieth-century novelists not usually associated with Maupassant. In *Pierre et Jean*, Pierre's alienated misanthropy and masochistic exploration of family secrets and the topography and seascapes around Le Havre are curiously similar to Roquentin's existential anguish and denunciation of bourgeois ignominy in Sartre's *La Nausée* (published fifty years later in 1938 and also set in a town based on Le Havre). In *Fort comme la mort* and *Notre cœur*, the febrile love affairs and self-destructive jealousy of wealthy dilettantes and narcissistic salon hostesses become predominant (and somewhat wearisome) themes, just as they do a generation later in Proust's depiction of Swann, Odette and the Verdurin clan in *Du côté de chez Swann* (1913).

To concentrate exclusively on Maupassant's two or three most successfully realized novels therefore risks overlooking some other interesting aspects of his evolution as a novelist and his contribution to the genre which at the beginning of the last chapter we called the realist social novel. While it is patently impossible to offer in-depth studies of six novels in a short chapter, it is more feasible and useful to revisit Maupassant's conception of the genre, to study how his approach to fiction-writing developed, and to examine some key examples from a wider range of texts that show his innovations in terms of psychology, narrative technique and social themes. It is also illuminating to study some of his shortcomings (particularly as there is no critical consensus about them). As we have already seen, Maupassant produced poems, articles and short stories with extraordinary facility and

HONORÉ DE BALZAC (1799-1850)
(D'après une gravure du Musée Carnavalet).

Honoré de Balzac by an unknown artist, before 1911.

spontaneity, yet rapidly became dissatisfied with the demands of such intensive productivity. However, he aspired to write longer fiction from the outset of his career, beginning the work that became *Une Vie* in 1877–8, until (after significant delays and revisions) it was finally published in April 1883, selling 25,000 copies within a few months. No other novel took such laborious preparation: *Bel-Ami* and *Mont-Oriol* appeared at two-year intervals (1885 and 1887), and *Pierre et Jean*, *Fort comme la mort* and *Notre coeur* annually (1888, 1889, 1890).

Whereas Maupassant wrote no theoretical reflections about the short story in terms of genre or personal craft, his many essays on novels and novelists offer insights that provide a useful starting point for this discussion. In an article entitled 'L'Évolution du roman au XIXe siècle' (1889), he declines to trace the long history of narrative fiction (which some historians claim preceded Graeco-Roman literature by several millennia in ancient Egypt).[1] He also passes over medieval chivalric romances and their modern successors, the lengthy (and immensely popular) adventure stories of Soulié, Sue and Dumas senior (while conceding that the latter was a *conteur de génie*, a veritable 'volcano erupting books'). For such *amuseurs* contribute little to 'literary art': what interests him are writers of a more philosophical bent who have developed the modern *roman de moeurs*.[2] Twenty-first-century readers may find this dismissal of so-called entertainers misguided, since it undervalues the creative power and appeal of the imagination which writers like Dumas, Verne and Maupassant himself exemplify; one suspects that Maupassant's yearning to be taken seriously as a novelist and commentator reveals a misunderstanding of his own natural talent as a storyteller.

Although his frame of reference is entirely French, Maupassant does not remind us that *Madame Bovary* (which he cites as a model of realistic observation and stylistic precision) is subtitled *moeurs de province*. In other words, the modern novel does more than depict universal human passions: it also offers an ethnographic account of local mores and manners, of people interacting in specific, historically situated social groups, of human behaviour in the widest sense (including areas considered shameful or unmentionable). The didacticism of earlier writers like Rousseau, Chateaubriand and Sand is also outmoded: fictional characters are no longer 'personified theses' advocating their authors' doctrines, but living, autonomous creations (Maupassant cites Prevost's *Manon Lescaut* (1731) as an admirable precursor with its 'prodigious analysis of the female heart'). The best contemporary novelists (such as the Goncourt brothers, Daudet and Zola) combine the quest for verisimilitude (which demands accurately documented observation of a particular milieu) with literary artistry and a quasi-scientific sensitivity to the manifold nuances of perception and existence. Their younger successors, however, seem less interested in the external world than in the hidden impulses and intricacies of the self (whether perceived as soul, heart or instincts). To avoid the potential monotony likely to result from concentrating exclusively on egocentric figures indifferent to consensual reality, they feel obliged to investigate degenerate selves increasingly detached from normal emotions and desires, 'inoculated with the mysterious viruses of all mental illnesses'.[3] Maupassant does not name specific writers or novels, but an obvious example would be Huysmans' *A rebours* (1884), whose aristocratic protagonist attempts to live out his decadent, aesthetic fantasies by creating a parallel world through his imagination.

Although all Maupassant's novels are set in a crisply delineated spatio-temporal reality derived from authentic, recognizable social settings in mid-nineteenth-century France (with none of the fantastic or mysterious elements that dominate many of the stories), critics have noted that, in the course of six novels, his fictional world undergoes a process of contraction, which affects space, time, plot, characters and narration.[4] The process can be seen either as bold and innovative, showing a concentration and internalization of perspective (moving away from objective reportage to explore the subjective and unconscious) or, less positively, as a diminution of his imaginative power and empathy, even ultimately as a facile, snobbish attempt to appeal to a small class of wealthy readers. The success or failure of this narrowing of perspective is in fact the main area of critical disagreement about Maupassant's later fiction.

Une Vie, as the title proclaims, is a fictional biography of an unhappy woman (like Flaubert's *Madame Bovary*), covering three decades from late adolescence to premature old age. While set earlier in the century during the Restoration and July Monarchy (like Flaubert's novel), political events play no part in Jeanne's strangely passive existence, although in recording her aristocratic family's financial mismanagement and social demotion, *Une Vie* accurately charts the decline of the provincial nobility. Whereas Emma Bovary never achieves her dreams of visiting Paris or exotic locales, Jeanne does enjoy a sensual awakening on honeymoon in Corsica, although this merely emphasizes the bitter disappointments and betrayals brought by her return to Normandy. In *Bel-Ami*, Maupassant creates a protagonist who is far more dynamic and successful than Jeanne or indeed any other character in his novels. In little more than three years, Georges Duroy (whose parents are peasants who run a café and smallholding in Normandy) is transformed from an impecunious clerk in a railway office into a wealthy journalist with an aristocratic title, married to the daughter of a powerful newspaper proprietor, financier and politician. Summarized so baldly, this metamorphosis sounds utterly implausible; perhaps what is most impressive about *Bel-Ami* is Maupassant's persuasive and compelling depiction of the Parisian press and wealthy bourgeoisie that facilitate Duroy's transformation (alongside his extraordinary ability to seduce women able to gratify and extend his inexhaustible desires and ambitions).

Like *Une Vie* and *Bel-Ami*, *Mont-Oriol* is a panoramic novel (in other words, the central characters are situated in a richly peopled social setting and detailed description of their interactions with this external world occupies most of the text). All three novels present a wide range of well-observed characters (from aristocrats to peasants), although unlike Maupassant's other novels, *Mont-Oriol* does not have a single dominant central character whose perspective shapes the narrative. As the title suggests, the novel is primarily about a place, or the creation of a commercial enterprise in a geological environment. This lack of individual psychological focus perhaps explains the book's relative neglect, although as Louis Forestier observes, it is Maupassant's most deliberately comic novel (any humour in his later works being entirely incidental).[5] The action however is reduced to little more than a year and limited to the diverse community that passes through the nascent Auvergne spa.

While these three earlier novels focus on individuals within communities (the rural aristocracy, the Parisian press, the patients, doctors and entrepreneurs who form a health spa), Maupassant's documentary interest in collective institutions is largely abandoned in his final novels. Louis Forestier calls *Pierre et Jean* an 'affront to naturalism' – that is, a blunt rejection of Zola's fictional practice of accurately situating particular groups and individuals within significant social institutions (such as mining, prostitution, agriculture, finance, the military and so forth) by focusing instead on 'one man's psychology'.[6] Although Pierre is nominally a doctor, his only patient in practice is himself. Deeply troubled when his younger brother Jean receives a substantial legacy from a deceased family friend, Pierre is unable to prevent his envious resentment ruining both his professional ambitions and personal relations with his brother and mother (never actually discovering whether Jean was the illegitimate son of his benefactor). This little novel was written in three months, about the same period of time as it takes for Pierre's complacent existence to implode financially, morally and emotionally.

Maupassant's assertion in the essay 'Le Roman' (published with *Pierre et Jean*) that he prefers objective novels where psychology is concealed (or revealed indirectly through action and behaviour) to analytical novels (where the narrator laboriously explores the innermost workings of a character's thoughts and feelings) is thus oddly contradicted by this novel and its two successors (as though again he had not fully grasped his reversion to a more traditional type of fiction focused on the self).[7] *Pierre et Jean* arguably melds both types through Pierre's inward and outward perspective (he analyses both his inner motives and other people and places), since it is written in the third person (as opposed to the more restrictive use of the first person in celebrated novels that explore the tortuous working of subjective consciousness, such as Constant's *Adolphe* (1816), Fromentin's *Dominique* (1862), Dujardin's *Les Lauriers sont coupés* (1888) or indeed Sartre's *La Nausée*). Louis Forestier argues that in *Pierre et Jean*, Maupassant 'is no longer interested in a story, of whatever kind, but in an interior story'; therefore 'the point of view ceases to be that of an omniscient narrator and is transferred to the partial and fragmented vision of one of the characters.'[8] This rather overstates the shift, since for example a key chapter shows a confrontation between Jean and his mother (from which Pierre is excluded) that reveals the details of her adultery to Jean and the reader (who thus do not share Pierre's continuing uncertainty about a vital element in the plot). And purely material external details do in fact continue to play an important part in the story; Pierre's relationships with other people are largely determined by money, for instance.

On the other hand, *Fort comme la mort* and *Notre coeur* generally dispense with the plot devices and material concerns that shape the action of the previous novels. Both books deal with unhappy amorous relationships among members of the wealthy bourgeoisie and aristocracy, whose tormented dalliances are treated with a sentimental earnestness strangely remote from the sarcastic disdain which Maupassant had expressed for affairs of the heart a decade earlier (remarking that love was as foolish and self-deceiving as religion).[9] In both cases, two prosperous and stable couples, formed outside conventional marriage but bound by genuine affection, are torn apart by the man's perverse or frustrated desires. In *Fort comme la mort*, an ageing society painter develops a quasi-incestuous passion for his mistress's adolescent daughter and is driven to suicide. In *Notre coeur*, the indolent hero resolves his disappointment with his mistress's lack of sexual passion and irksome independence less melodramatically and more pragmatically, by adopting an unsophisticated servant girl as a concurrent, subordinate lover who proves more sensually and emotionally gratifying. But the ironic or cynical detachment which Maupassant usually adopts towards his characters' foibles and misfortunes is strangely lacking in these final novels, despite (or possibly because of) their extraordinarily privileged existence and somewhat futile *marivaudages* (mannered flirtations). Indeed, the narrator's fascination with the narcissistic self-absorption of these insipid *mondains* at times displays a 'core of sentimental snobbery', a connivance verging on the abject.[10]

While the titles *Fort comme la mort* and *Notre coeur* are intended to imply a universality of suffering through love, which the thematic and formal narrowness of these works singularly fails to convey, Maupassant's first novel, *Une Vie* (translated as *A Woman's Life*), does inspire empathy and pathos, as the innocent heroine endures an unceasing series of misfortunes and betrayals. Although she is the daughter of a baron and marries a viscount, Jeanne des Vauds is completely lacking in aristocratic *hauteur* or even Emma Bovary's petty bourgeois callousness and egotism. Whereas Mme Bovary's frantic quest for self-gratification ultimately drives her to suicide and ruins her family, Jeanne is a victim of her naivety and good nature. Emma neglects her daughter, who ends up working in a mill; Jeanne is impoverished by her son's improvidence. But if the characters of *Une Vie* are often either quietly sympathetic (like Jeanne's elderly relatives) or memorably overdrawn (notably the fanatical abbé Tolbiac, and the murderous comte de Fourville, who hurls his adulterous spouse and Jeanne's husband over a cliff when he discovers them consorting in a shepherd's wheeled hut), the novel is problematic in other ways.

Extant manuscripts reveal that Maupassant struggled over several years to improve the novel's structural cohesion and to step outside Flaubert's shadow, not only in the portrayal of Jeanne, but in episodes, descriptive passages and stylistic mannerisms that potentially made the work read like a pastiche of *Madame Bovary*. This meant a substantial amount of cutting: of minor characters (only the self-effacing Aunt Lison survives), but also of Jeanne's lecherous brother Henry (her philandering husband Julien and feckless son Paul acquire his libidinous temperament). A chapter where Jeanne adopts a blind boy tormented by other children was also removed, probably because a hideously mutilated blind beggar haunts Emma Bovary's final moments. Yet Jeanne herself remains a partial amalgam of Emma and Mme Aubain from Flaubert's affecting tale 'Un coeur simple' ('A Simple Heart/Soul', about a widow who loses both her children and is comforted by her faithful servant Félicité). On the other hand, Jeanne's long-suffering servant Rosalie (who bears a son by Jeanne's husband) is a far more dominant figure than Félicité, while Jeanne's resigned passivity (what Forestier calls an 'absence of being'[11]) is remote from Emma's fiery impulsiveness, even if they share the same convent education and romantic reveries.

Among the most appealing features of Maupassant's fiction are his impressionistic descriptions of landscapes and seascapes, in which *Une Vie* is pleasingly abundant. Here too the novel inevitably echoes *Madame Bovary*, given the shared Norman setting (in bravura descriptions of the approaches to Rouen, for example, or of country horse-riding as a stimulating preamble to adulterous coupling). Louis Forestier observes that 'Normandy is not evoked for its picturesque charm; it forms an inner landscape.'[12] The presence of the natural world, the physical environment, is not gratuitous (or threateningly contingent, as it is in Sartre's *La Nausée*), but a determining factor in a character's existential equilibrium; it may have a positive or negative impact on Maupassant's characters, according to their circumstances and temperament. In Jeanne's case, the initial, easy intimacy of the association suggests her innocence, vulnerability and isolation from close human contact. Thus unwelcome heavy rainfall is described as 'the first deep sorrow of her existence', whereas a brilliant sunrise fills her with rapture: 'and Jeanne felt her herself becoming mad with happiness. A delirious joy, an infinite tenderness for the splendour of things drowned her swooning heart. It was her sun! Her dawn! The rising of her hopes!' Intoxicated by a boat trip, she feels that 'only three things were truly beautiful in creation: light, space and water.'[13] Her sensual pleasure in swimming alone far out to sea contrasts with the physical and moral repugnance she experiences when Julien brutally deflowers her. Only in the torrid climate of Corsica does she briefly experience sexual pleasure, before her husband's infidelity, avarice and drunkenness lead to their estrangement.

Her renewed isolation is conveyed by a much bleaker perception of nature and humanity. Thus winter light 'stains her bed with blood' and the rising sun is 'bloated like a drunkard's face'.[14] Recycling an image used in a letter to his mother (quoted in Chapter One), Maupassant writes that 'December passed slowly, the black month, a dark hole at the bottom of the year.'[15] Her discovery of incontrovertible proof of Julien's adultery with her friend revolts her, provoking a Flaubertian aphorism: 'sometimes one weeps for one's illusions with as much sadness as for the dead.'[16] But as she loses her husband, the affection of her son, her ageing parents and the family fortune, Jeanne is shrouded by what Forestier calls 'a foggy atmosphere', entombed within 'empty duration', sinking into reclusive lethargy and self-pity.[17] Her faithful companion Rosalie (whose expectations have been lower and life much harder) points out others are worse off; finally, Jeanne's incipient old age is temporarily brightened by their adoption of her grandchild after Paul's wife dies in childbirth. The novel ends with Rosalie offering the homely maxim: 'life, you see, is never as good or bad as you think.'[18] This too is a paraphrase of a comment by Flaubert to Maupassant in a letter of 18 December 1878, leading Forestier to interpret it as heavily ironical (since both women's lives have been blighted by most standards). Yet Flaubert's dictum is itself a paraphrase of La Rochefoucauld's 49th maxim, 'one is never as happy or as unhappy as one imagines', suggesting perhaps that Rosalie's practical humanity is preferable to either Jeanne's resigned torpor or Emma Bovary's self-destructive frenzy.[19]

Une Vie is a Flaubertian novel both in its preoccupation with failure and disappointment and stylistic mannerisms, such as melancholic aphorisms, ternary phrases and slightly strained metaphors. Thus we are told of Jeanne's parents that kindness 'dried up money in their hands as the sun dries up the water in a marsh. It flowed, fled and disappeared.'[20] While *Bel-Ami* is also much preoccupied with cash flow and liquidity (as are *Mont-Oriol* and *Pierre et Jean*), it is primarily a novel about conquest and success. Whereas many well-known novels about *arrivistes* who aspire to worldly success and social promotion actually depict their eventual failure (from Stendhal's *Le Rouge et le noir* (1830), Balzac's *Illusions perdues* (1837–43), Flaubert's *L'Éducation sentimentale* (1869), Hardy's *Jude the Obscure* (1895) to Tom Wolfe's *Bonfire of the Vanities* (1987)), *Bel-Ami* ends with Georges Duroy's consecration as a sort of secular messiah (making him unique among Maupassant's fictional protagonists).

Since the other novels and many stories show characters mostly thwarted in their aspirations by circumstance and temperament, *Bel-Ami* raises the interesting question: how is success defined and achieved, and at what cost? The first part of the novel in particular provides a meticulously detailed and fascinating answer, in both a material and moral sense. When the novel starts, Duroy is a friendless clerk earning 1,500 francs a year and living in a dingy garret, with literally only 3 francs and 40 centimes in his pocket, and enraged at the frustration of his appetites. A chance encounter with an ex-army comrade who has become a journalist allows him to rapidly improve his professional, financial and sexual prospects: as a trainee reporter his salary doubles, he encounters rich and influential people, and his seductive charm beguiles a wealthy society lady eager to satisfy his sexual and monetary needs. Her young daughter Laurine nicknames him 'Bel-Ami', which has no obvious English equivalent (neither literal nor idiomatic translations – 'fine friend', 'fancy man', 'lover boy', 'charmer' – quite convey the caddish attractiveness it suggests).

Duroy follows his mentor Forestier's advice to adopt the appearance and demeanour of the wealthy elite. This involves, for example, acquiring formal evening dress. Having previously exchanged his hussar's uniform for a civilian's ready-made suit costing 60 francs, without shedding his subordinate status, Duroy hires a tailcoat and is astounded when he sees the reflection of a debonair toff in a full-length mirror and belatedly recognizes himself. But the transformation involves more than tailoring and acting the part of a man about town: to succeed, Duroy has to acquire new professional and personal skills and effectively modify his personality (acquiring a more sophisticated *savoir-faire* and *savoir-vivre*, even if his predatory impulses remain dominant). When later on he visits his elderly parents in Normandy, they too fail to recognize him or to bridge the social and cultural gulf which he has crossed. As we saw in a previous chapter, Maupassant felt obliged to placate outraged colleagues by disingenuously denying that the opportunistic Duroy had any talent as a journalist, a denial which other critics of the novel often dutifully echo.[21] But this is not what *Bel-Ami* actually shows us in Duroy's gradual but remarkable cultural adaptation, if one traces his progress more attentively. Having shone at the Forestiers' dinner party with his tales of French Algeria, he is invited to write an article for the newspaper *La Vie française*, but is utterly unable to do so until Madeleine Forestier obligingly turns his paltry efforts into a polished piece (it seems she provides the same service for her husband). A second article written alone is rejected and Duroy realizes he needs to bide his time. Unlike his author, Duroy is without literary genius, but so too are most media folk. But he is ideally suited to the needs of the newspaper, which serves to promote the business and financial interests of its owner Walter and his associates. Indeed we are told that Duroy 'soon became a remarkable reporter, sure of his

Édouard Manet, *A Bar at the Folies-Bergère*, 1882, oil on canvas. The Folies-Bergère was the famous dance hall featured in *Bel-Ami*.

information, shrewd, quick and subtle, a real asset for the paper'
and that by writing the gossip column, he acquires 'a skill with his
pen and tact which he lacked when he wrote his second article'.[22]

Madeleine advises him to cultivate the director's wife and he is
soon promoted to 'chef des Échos' (head of gossip and off-the-record
news, a more influential position than this title suggests). By the
end of part one, he has become 'a skilful and perceptive political
writer', even if he still has trouble finding ideas and is financially
dependent on Mme de Marelle (whose wealthy husband he astutely
befriends).[23] His naive joy at publishing an article and seducing
a society lady is overshadowed by his resentful awareness that he
is still remote from real wealth, power and status. In the second
part of the novel, Duroy attains these goals by unscrupulously and
ruthlessly exploiting the three women to whom he is successively
attached. After his mentor's death, Duroy takes over Forestier's
job, and by marrying Madeleine, his widow and apartment; his
colleagues and Laurine sarcastically nickname him 'Forestier', their
assumption that Duroy is the inferior partner in this marriage
perhaps explaining his rancorous posthumous dislike of Forestier
and suspicion towards Madeleine. After discovering that he has
been duped both by the newspaper proprietor Walter and by
Madeleine, Duroy eventually engineers his revenge: skilfully
manipulating the law and social convention in his favour, he
divorces Madeleine, after ruining the career of the minister who
was her lover, and elopes with Walter's daughter Suzanne, obliging
his boss to accept him as a son-in-law to avoid further scandal. By
the end of the novel, Duroy is editor-in-chief and looking forward to
becoming 'one of the masters of the earth' in finance and politics.[24]

While Walter admires Duroy's brilliance as a seducer and
intriguer (seeing the consummate roguery behind his respectable
facade as an indispensable qualification for political success),[25] the
mistresses whose affection and purses he shamelessly purloins raise
more conventional objections to his behaviour. For the unfortunate

Mme Walter, maddened by jealousy when spurned by Duroy in favour of her daughter, he is 'the vilest being I know'.[26] Mme de Marelle is equally indignant, denouncing not merely his cynical manipulation of women but his pompous hypocrisy: 'you deceive everybody, you exploit everybody, you steal pleasure and money everywhere, and you expect me to treat you like an honest man?'[27] His response to her accusations is to give her a violent beating. Yet just as Mme de Marelle (who has no scruples about deceiving her own spouse) is always reconciled with Duroy, the novel's economy and satirical perspective also basically support and justify his predatory behaviour as a necessary adaptation to this particular social environment. *Bel-Ami* is a fictional demonstration of Maupassant's assertion in his 1884 essay 'Le Fond du coeur' that conventional morality is a mask covering most people's essential egoism and dishonesty. Apart from the child Laurine, all the central characters are as self-serving and unscrupulous as Bel-Ami and usually well aware of this; indeed, Mme Walter's self-deceiving and quasi-blasphemous religious devotions (leading her to confuse an image of Christ with Duroy) are arguably more repellent than the knowing manipulation of conventions practised by Madeleine, Mme de Marelle and Walter.

Critics sometimes argue that Duroy is condemned or subverted more obliquely. Douglas Parmée suggests that success is achieved mainly through 'wily mediocrity' (duping one's benefactors and friends) and ambition shown to be basically futile: 'success is ultimately futile because of the ephemerality of all life.'[28] A few metaphysical episodes certainly insist on the fragility and transience of existence: the description of Forestier's grim decline and death, Duroy's uncharacteristic brooding before a duel, the elderly poet Norbert de Varennes' melancholic laments. But these are largely parenthetical interludes, which broaden the novel's perspective without halting the hero's advancement. Gérard Delaisement objects that politics in *Bel-Ami* 'is too often reduced to embezzlement raised into a state institution'.[29] A key background element of the plot involves the French government's decision to annex Morocco, which allows Walter and his cronies to enjoy enormous profits by surreptitiously acquiring Moroccan assets and resources in advance of the invasion. The episode is skilfully calqued on recent French adventures (or misadventures) in Tonkin, Egypt and Tunisia, and accurately represents Third Republic venality and opportunism in the 1880s, however caricatural and limited Maupassant's account of contemporary politicians may be. The closing paragraphs of the novel show the triumphant Duroy (who now styles himself Baron Du Roy) intoxicated by joy looking towards the Chamber of Deputies as a future site of conquest, enjoying an epiphany uncontaminated by any fears or doubts.

Bel-Ami has an exemplary crispness, clarity and vitality in its celebratory account of Duroy's metamorphosis, abounding with telling descriptive details that convey the sensual and material delight brought by his progress from poverty to luxury (such as his pleasurable astonishment when sinking for the first time into a padded armchair at the Forestiers'). Its compelling account of sexual and political intrigue and ambition makes it a Balzacian novel that is largely stripped of Balzac's digressive verbosity, unintelligible financial computations and melodramatic plot contrivances. Although presented almost entirely from Duroy's viewpoint, it has an extensive range of memorable secondary characters, even if some key supporting figures (like Madeleine, Mme de Marelle and Walter) are relatively underdeveloped. We learn that Walter, for example, is a multi-dimensional figure, a 'deputy, financier, business and money man, Jew and southerner, director of *La Vie française*' and father of two marriageable daughters, but he is shown playing only the last of these multiple roles.[30]

Mont-Oriol attempts to remedy these deficiencies, in that two dominant figures among the central group of characters are the wealthy Jewish financier William Andermatt and his wife Christiane, daughter of the impoverished Marquis de Ravenel. The novel has three interlinked strands, which can be summed up as financial and social, personal and psychological, and topographical and geological. The first strand (arguably the most interesting) describes Andermatt's successful struggle to launch a new spa by buying and developing the land owned by the Oriols, a wily peasant clan. The second deals with more intimate human relations, particularly Christiane's impassioned love affair with her brother Gontran's wealthy friend Paul Brétigny. Christiane gives birth to his child, but Paul expediently follows Gontran by marrying into the Oriol family. The third describes in often lyrical detail the volcanic landscapes of the Auvergne (which Maupassant knew well from the regular cures he took at the spa of Châtelguyon in the mid-1880s) and their varying impact on these characters. *Mont-Oriol* is oddly ignored by many readers and critics, since to my mind, the book's diversity and exploration of an unfamiliar, provincial setting make it far more readable and worthy of attention than Maupassant's later novels set in Parisian high society.

As Roy Porter observes, the burgeoning consumer society of the nineteenth century made hydrotherapy and spa treatments 'big business, promising elegant healing rituals, social contacts and rich pickings for hoteliers and doctors', although the therapeutic benefits of being violently flushed with mineral water either internally or externally seem to be mostly imaginary or psychosomatic.[31] *Mont-Oriol* makes it perfectly clear that Maupassant – and the more perceptive characters – suspect that, however fashionable, such enterprises are based on quackery and gullibility (although both author and characters nonetheless stoically endure unpleasant, invasive treatments). Much of the book's unexpected humour derives from such contradictions. In the opening chapter, Christiane and her family circle are sojourning in the spa village of Enval, which attracts few clients, despite being open for six years and possessing a spring that is capable of curing all ills (according to one of the competing, Molièresque doctors whose self-important mendacity provides comic rather than medical relief).

When old Oriol blows up a large rock obstructing his land (the destruction of this landmark attracting a large crowd of onlookers, such is the monotony of provincial life), the explosion unexpectedly exposes an unknown mineral spring, whose geological and financial possibilities are rapidly grasped by Andermatt after he consults an engineer. The blast incidentally kills a curious dog, despite Brétigny's foolhardy attempt to rescue it. Christiane is impressed by his bravery, as he intended, but soils herself by treading in the animal's remains (perhaps a symbolic reflection of their future relationship). While Andermatt remains blind to his wife's frustration and eventual infidelity, his outstanding talents as a businessman and financier are adroitly demonstrated in parallel to her emotional and sensual awakening. The technical details of his negotiation of the purchase, development and promotion of the spring are presented interestingly and intelligibly, and enlivened by the comical rivalry between Parisian sophisticates and obtuse peasant cunning.

For example, Oriol and his brutish son consider their spring 'like an animal put up for sale',[32] for which one drives a hard bargain, confirmed by tangible evidence such as written documents, and they have no comprehension of Andermatt's grandiose aspirations to turn gushing water into vast streams of cash, which in turn sustain an enterprise and dependent community, deemed by the government to be a public utility. They bribe an old poacher who pretends to be paralysed, to promote the spring's healing powers by simulating a miraculous recovery (he subsequently relapses in order to refresh this source of income). Within a year, the new station is attracting hundreds of patients and takes over its failing nearby rival. By encouraging his brother-in-law Gontran and friend Paul to marry Oriol's nubile daughters, Andermatt effectively gains control of the wealthy peasants' land. His alliance with Christiane's aristocratic family is equally opportunistic, opening up new markets for the Jewish banker in return for covering the family's debts. When Andermatt complains about their spendthrift ways, both his amiable father-in-law and wastrel brother-in-law condescendingly tell him that hoarding and penny-pinching are not a sign of nobility. While objecting to such anti-Semitic jibes, Andermatt admits to Count Gontran that their relationship is based on mercenary complicity:

> You reproach me with being a Jew, that is, with earning money, with avariciousness, with speculating that verges on fraud. Now, my dear fellow, I'm forever lending you this money which takes me a lot of trouble to earn, in other words giving it to you.[33]

When Louis Forestier asserts that 'there is no anti-Semitism in Maupassant's work', the hostility expressed towards Jewish businessmen in *Bel-Ami* and *Mont-Oriol* shows this defensive claim is manifestly untrue.[34] There is however no reason to suppose that the author's accurate recording of unsympathetic characters' social prejudices reflects Maupassant's own views.

Andermatt's tactical brilliance as a financier and negotiator does however necessitate accepting compromises in personal relations that seem rather demeaning, notably his studied tolerance of his in-laws' condescension and unawareness that his wife has a lover and their child was fathered by this lover (Christiane's unlikely claim to be pregnant nearly a year before she gives birth is left unexplained). Christiane's sensual and emotional arousal from her marital lethargy is stimulated not merely by Brétigny's seductive charm, but by the unexpected sense of well-being and happiness she derives from plunging body and soul into the mineral baths and landscape.[35] Paul further enchants her by invoking other senses and arts (smell, music, poetry); when they embrace by a ruined château in moonlight, we are told 'he took her as easily as plucking a ripe fruit',[36] a simile favoured by Maupassant which implies that erotic consummation is no more than the gratification of a basic appetite. Indeed, Brétigny has the 'soul of a modern Don Quixote',[37] and is soon repelled by her pregnancy (which he considers a defilement of romantic ideals and sexual pleasure).[38] Hence his ready willingness to transfer his affections to Charlotte Oriol and capricious proposal of marriage. But their betrothal is more than a whim: apart from the fact they are wealthy heiresses, the two sisters' social promotion through marriage into the aristocracy and upper bourgeoisie is the outcome of Oriol's deliberate decision to have them educated in a convent and trained in social graces. The bitter rivalry and jealousy which Louise and Charlotte briefly experience when the cynical Gontran flirts with both of them is resolved when Paul joins the quartet; finer feelings are less important than the exchange of financial and social capital which the marriages achieve. On the other hand, Christiane's painful confinement is accompanied by an equally painful sense of abandonment and loss; but finally she too is obliged to accept Paul's betrayal and her husband's blinkered self-satisfaction. However, while she finds some consolation in maternity, Brétigny is denied access to their daughter and his hurried marriage is described as a 'trap of destiny'.[39] The compromises and deceptions needed for success in business are thus paralleled by similar pragmatism in human relations. This allows the central characters in *Mont-Oriol* to achieve at least some of their aspirations, with nobody left utterly bereft or triumphant. Perhaps this balanced outcome reflects the fact the novel is essentially about a place and a social group in harmony with its environment, rather than the frustrated individuals at odds with their family or intimate circle and surroundings who dominate all the other novels.

Certainly Pierre Roland, the misanthropic protagonist of *Pierre et Jean*, is totally devoid of the tact and finesse which allow

Andermatt to resolve conflict and dissonance in his extended family (he even diplomatically attributes his belated paternity to the rejuvenating power of the Oriols' spring).[40] Pierre's blundering attempts to uncover a long-hidden family secret are both unsuccessful and destructive. His quest produces family breakdown and nothing else, with the legitimate son Pierre sent into exile but still ignorant of his brother's true paternity. The younger brother Jean is empowered by his biological father Maréchal's legacy (enabling him to launch his career as a lawyer and marry a prosperous young widow), but alienated from the inoffensive man he now realizes is his stepfather. Yet Pierre perceives himself as a virtuous seeker after truth, contemptuous of the complacent hypocrisy and commonplace pastimes which sustain his family. He is also intermittently aware of the malevolent aspects of his own personality (such as arrogance, envy and a quasi-incestuous attachment to his mother). At its best, the novel invests Pierre's tormented quest with a tragic intensity that inventively resurrects and plausibly domesticates the bloodthirsty family feuds and fraternal enmity of Greek myth and the Old Testament in the mundane environment of Le Havre.

This is no doubt why many critics consider *Pierre et Jean* to be Maupassant's best novel, perhaps a backhanded compliment, since it is really an extended novella in its almost exclusive focus on Pierre's reaction to a momentous event.[41] As Robert Lethbridge notes, Pierre's introspection and reflective capacity 'differentiate him from the unthinking mediocrity of those around him', even if his perception is often distorted and his superiority seems self-interested and unmerited.[42] Maupassant summarily abandons the principle of narratorial impersonality and detachment adumbrated in his essays on Flaubert and the novel. Lethbridge argues that Pierre's psychological complexity requires a more analytical perspective, focused on his mental states. The problem is however that the narrator does not merely share Pierre's subjective ruminations (in the sense of communicating them at length to the reader), but apparently agrees with his bleak judgements and self-pitying laments (there is a similar lack of objectivity in the last two novels). For example, we are bluntly informed that the interior decoration in Jean's new apartment is 'pretentious and fussy', clearly an observation illustrating Pierre's seething resentment, but one with which the narrator apparently concurs.[43] Yet on rereading the book, after one has grasped the basic plot and family dynamics, one is inclined to take a far more critical attitude towards the protagonist and his dilemma. It is hard to avoid the conclusion that he is essentially a melancholic loafer and self-centred prig, whose scornful judgements about his family and few friends reveal an incapacitating lack of empathy with other people.

That Pierre can be interpreted in a way that runs against the narrator's sympathetic treatment of him is not necessarily a defect (one might argue that despite himself, Maupassant cannot help ironizing his character's situation, showing it to be other than he imagines). But this biased perspective does distort the presentation of the subordinate characters in his orbit, who risk, as it were, being drawn into the black hole of his misanthropy. For example, having belatedly qualified as a doctor at the age of thirty, Pierre is still entirely dependent on his father, a retired jeweller, yet the latter is always treated as a caricatural nonentity and condescendingly referred to as 'père Roland' rather than by his forename, whereas the fact his son is a shameless sponger is barely noticed. Jean is five years younger, equally idle and dependent, but of a more amiable, easy-going disposition. Throughout the novel, old Roland remains complacently unaware of the growing tension between the brothers and their mother, for 'he was one of those people unperturbed by anything'.[44]

The brothers' latent rivalry takes at first a relatively innocent form when they put on a rowing display to impress the widow

Mme Rosémilly, but Pierre lacks the stamina of his stronger half-brother (ironically, Jean's placidity resembles that of his adoptive father). Jean's substantial legacy (worth two and a half times as much as old Roland's comfortable pension) allows him to defeat Pierre in their contest to rent a luxurious apartment and to win the widow's hand; eventually Jean decides that Pierre's intolerable treatment of their mother means that the older brother must quit the family and Le Havre for good. In *Bel-Ami*, Duroy's pretence of shock at his wife Madeleine's receipt of a similar legacy from her benefactor is simply a cynical ploy to extort half the money from her. Pierre is incapable of such tactics, but his supposed concern with defending the family honour barely masks spite and envy, as he is well aware. He is an impractical dreamer: telling Jean he wants to leave on a ship and explore the world (but unwilling to ask Jean for a share of the legacy to fund the voyage), he then determines to make a fortune from wealthy patients, without ever making any attempt to set up a medical practice.

The two friends Pierre has outside the family circle immediately perceive the implication of the anomalous legacy (that is, the wealthy bachelor Maréchal was Mme Roland's lover and Jean is their son), although Pierre at first dismisses this interpretation from a waitress whom he pays for sex as 'an infamy'.[45] While recognizing the mercenary nature of human relations, Pierre is reluctant to admit his mother behaved like everyone else (including himself). He tracks down a portrait of Maréchal which his mother has concealed, although her agitation is more revealing than the picture. But his obnoxious behaviour towards both his parents makes any frank confrontation between Pierre and his mother impossible: she finally confesses the truth to Jean. While the narrator oddly contrasts Jean's 'somnolent nature' with Pierre's 'secret dignity', a less biased interpretation shows Jean simply to be sensible and pragmatic.[46] He accepts the legacy, consoles his mother, and is unperturbed to learn that old Roland is not his biological father, since 'for a very long time he had suffered unconsciously at feeling himself the child of this easy-going dimwit' (although this further condemnation of Roland does not really correspond to Jean's blander temperament).[47]

Finally, Pierre is given a modest post as a ship's doctor (through professional connections rather than any initiative on his part). Although this fulfils his yearning to travel and escape a milieu from which he is totally estranged, Pierre is nonetheless sunk into a 'cesspit of misery',[48] seeing himself condemned to the 'life of a roaming convict, entirely because his mother had submitted to the caresses of her lover'.[49] We are told the bunk in his well-appointed cabin resembles a coffin, although in fact he enjoys the opulent surroundings of first-class travellers rather than the stinking squalor of emigrants in steerage. In the opening chapter, Roland points out, as the family returns contentedly from a boating expedition, the arrival of a ship outlined by the setting sun: 'over the sea, stretched flat like a piece of blue cloth, immense and gleaming with gold and fire, a black cloud could be seen rising against the pink sky, in the direction he indicated.'[50] In the final chapter, this optimistic image is reversed, as the gloomy Pierre departs on a liner called *Lorraine* (after the province annexed by the victorious Germans in 1871), that diminishes 'as though it had melted into the ocean'.[51] But the reluctant exile's disappearance does little to diminish the celebratory mood of the rest of the family.

There are passages in *Pierre et Jean* describing Pierre's anguished nocturnal wanderings through Le Havre which anticipate Roquentin's bouts of existential alienation in Sartre's *La Nausée*. Thus the streets are 'shrouded in fog which made the night heavy, opaque and noisome. It was as if a pestilential smoke had enveloped the earth.'[52] Reality dissolves as it impinges on a distressed consciousness, but in Maupassant's case, he makes it clear that the process is metaphorical in writing 'On eût dit': the ultimate solidity and objective reality of the external world are not challenged in

Passenger ship docking at Le Havre around 1890.

Maupassant's novels, even though he emphasizes how illusory
or partial subjective experience may be. Pierre vanishes from the
novel, but the sea and land remain untouched; the natural world
is independent of human consciousness, and his immediate social
circle barely registers his exclusion. In other words, Maupassant
retains the basic conventions of literary realism: even when he
makes a character's mental and emotional inner life the central
element in his novels, the character and narrative are firmly
situated in a consensual, spatio-temporal reality that determines
relations and behaviour. *Pierre et Jean* depicts this interaction of
self and world interestingly (that Pierre seems misguided and
egotistical rather than pitiful or unfortunate still involves the
reader engaging with the character's tormented dilemmas). It
is much harder to defend the last two completed novels, *Fort
comme la mort* and *Notre coeur*. Many of the writer's most faithful
commentators decline to do so.

Jean-Paul Sartre portrayed by Arturo Espinosa, 2013.

Louis Forestier remarks drily that *Fort comme la mort* 'does not enjoy a good reputation'.[53] Francis Steegmuller bluntly calls both novels 'lamentable',[54] and since they are often compared to Maupassant's friend and contemporary Paul Bourget's psychological high-life novels, throws in a damning assessment of Bourget for good measure.[55] Edward D. Sullivan notes that *Fort comme la mort* is about artistic sterility and decline and that its repetitive tedium ironically demonstrates the author's 'failing powers were not adequate to the task of portraying that decline in a novel'. As for *Notre coeur*, Sullivan finds it 'a formless mass of what seem like excerpts from essays, occasionally applied to one of the characters or uttered by one of them'.[56] Although other critics disagree, they are generally less persuasive (since they simply ignore glaring weaknesses in the construction of these final books). Thus André Vial praises *Fort comme la mort*'s innovative treatment of obsession, while curiously acknowledging Émile Henriot's unflattering opinion that it is maladroit and vacuous.[57]

Both novels lack conviction, in terms of style, plot, characterization and social settings, and offer few compensatory insights about love and art (if Maupassant anticipates Proust, it is in a very dilute fashion). Their rather cryptic titles betray a basic uncertainty about what they wish to communicate. In *Fort comme la mort*, the society painter Olivier Bertin has enjoyed a happy, adulterous relationship with his mistress, Countess Any de Guilleroy, for twelve years, untroubled by her husband, a worldly politician. This equilibrium is disturbed by the death of Any's mother and the blossoming of her daughter Annette, who becomes a more beautiful double of her mother, closely resembling a portrait done by Bertin which helped initiate their affair. This replication of her younger self intensifies the countess's fear of ageing and fascinates Bertin (Annette is not only her mother rejuvenated but a living version of the painting, an embodiment of his creative vitality in its former vigour). After his painting is meanly attacked in *Le Figaro* as hopelessly outmoded and he is kept away from her daughter by the countess, Bertin acknowledges the dangerous nature of his obsession: 'something irresistible, destructive, stronger than death. I'm possessed by it, like a burning house by fire!'[58]

As Louis Forestier observes, this single explicit reference to the novel's title is rather confusing.[59] The expression *Fort comme la mort* derives from the Song of Solomon (8:6): 'love is strong as death; jealousy is cruel as the grave: the coals thereof are coals of fire, which hath a most vehement flame.' Love is not *stronger* than death, as Bertin asserts, but *like* death, an inescapable, corrosive process leading to oblivion and extinction, a point stressed in the final sentence after Bertin dies in a street accident that appears to be suicide.[60] The faltering realization of this pessimistic parable is however likely to leave most readers unmoved or irritated by the characters' neurotic narcissism and the author's compliant attitude towards them. The title *Notre coeur* (Our Heart) similarly implies a sentimental complicity between the central characters and readers of the novel: their emotional frustrations and yearnings are universalized, assuming that we all experience them. But since twenty-first-century readers are highly unlikely to share the attitudes towards sexuality, gender and class evinced by the protagonists and narrator, their dilemmas may simply strike us as trivial or perverse.

Little purpose is served by enumerating the flaws of *Fort comme la mort* in detail; a few characteristic examples suffice to justify the negative judgements already cited about the failure of imagination and writing which this novel displays. Too often its attempts to communicate psychological depth are simply dull and trite. Both the painter Bertin and his mistress Any are neurotically obsessed by their fear of ageing, despite being healthy and rich; her daughter Annette blooms, but does little more than pose and simper throughout. The world-weary Bertin tells her how vacuous high society is: they are all 'mannequins' who 'simulate everything, even laughter'.[61] But far from satirizing these puppets, the narrator views them with a cloyingly sentimental sympathy, adopting a style adorned with clumsy romantic clichés: thus we are told Bertin's 'heart was hot and palpitating like a burning rag shaken in his chest'.[62] At no point does Maupassant attempt to describe Bertin's technique and craft as an artist; indeed, beyond light sketching, he never does any creative work, spending his time moping or frequenting wealthy socialites whom he despises. The most interesting parts of the novel are the set pieces which depict the cultural events attended by the social elite, such as a performance of Gounod's *Faust* and a Salon *vernissage*.

Notre coeur depicts a similar problematic relationship, between André Mariolle, a wealthy bachelor and dilettante, and a younger widow and society hostess Michèle de Burne. Since both these surnames have vulgar slang meanings, this is rather like calling characters Pratt and Balls in English; but the irreverent mockery which Maupassant directs at misguided or pretentious characters in his stories is completely absent from this final novel. Indeed, he generally adopts a tone of tragic solemnity which hardly seems justified by the characters' indolence, narcissism and extraordinarily privileged circumstances. Mariolle is supposedly a talented violinist and travel writer, but never actually plays a note or writes a word; his friends consider him to be 'a very amiable and intelligent failure'.[63] He is frustrated by Michèle's lack of sexual passion and worldly devotion to her salon with its *clan artiste* (although in fact she accepts him as a clandestine lover and treats him amicably and loyally). Indeed, her disinclination to surrender her sexual and social independence makes her a more dominant character than her doleful lover (reversing the power relationship of male philanderer and subordinate female characteristic of Maupassant's earlier fiction).[64]

Characteristics which twenty-first-century readers may find acceptable or even admirable are however presented by the narrator in his somewhat intrusive, didactic commentary as undesirable or perverse. While he accepts that Mme de Burne represents a novel version of the feminine, that her impenetrable narcissism (exemplified by the three-panelled mirror in which she encloses her image) is a source of charm and means to power, her self-inflicted ennui and egotistical philistinism are presented as typical female limitations. Thus having enticed the avant-garde sculptor Prédolé to her salon, she proves incapable of charming him or understanding his aesthetic theories and aspirations. Having been abused by her brutal husband during a traumatic marriage, she appears to be more attracted to women than men, but this bisexual theme is not developed. Michèle is certainly a more intriguing and robust character than the anaemic Mariolle, as are secondary figures like the sculptor Prédolé (usually seen as modelled on Rodin) and the novelist Gaston de Lamarthe (a self-portrait of Maupassant).

Apart from some magnificent descriptive passages (notably of the seascapes around Mont-Saint-Michel), *Notre coeur* is perhaps most interesting as a pallid anticipation of Proustian themes: the failure of love and artistic ambition, the perverse woman or object of desire who remains ungraspable, the futile *mondanités* which divert the wealthy. But it has none of Proust's aesthetic and philosophical ambitions, formal radicalism or satirical verve. It was serialized in the *Revue des deux mondes* in May and June 1890, a conservative review which Maupassant had previously rejected contemptuously as the enemy of innovative writing. It is difficult to avoid the conclusion that his career as a novelist ended rather ignominiously, particularly if one recalls that he left two further novels unfinished. The extant fragments of *L'Ame étrangère* and *L'Angélus* were published posthumously in 1894 and 1895. Maupassant planned to set *L'Ame étrangère* partly in Romania,

View of Mont-Saint-Michel, 2016.

but was unable to accept an invitation from the Queen to visit the country in 1889 and abandoned the project for *Notre coeur*; the central character Mariolle was retained, but what would have been a cosmopolitan novel became Parisian.[65] *L'Angélus* has a striking prologue set during the Franco-Prussian war, but Maupassant's failing health forced him to abandon the work in April 1891.

Failing health is however not an adequate explanation for the striking decline in Maupassant's creative powers as a novelist after the four impressive works he published from 1883 to 1888. In 1889 and 1890, for example, he was still able to produce some of his most compelling stories, such as 'Allouma', 'Mouche', 'Le Champ d'oliviers' and 'L'Inutile Beauté'. Apart from the obvious creative demands imposed by longer works of fiction, he was probably well aware that his attempts to reinvent himself as a psychological novelist revealed in practice a regression to the sort of conventional, conformist writing which he had repudiated in his critical essays. In the final chapters of this study, we will return to a broader perspective on his literary career, with an analysis of the world view communicated by his works and their legacy in the twentieth and twenty-first centuries.

6

Ironist

Many critics, biographers and readers of Maupassant have assumed that the cynical pessimism and desolate resignation conveyed by some of his fiction and personal correspondence accurately and adequately reflect the writer's own experience and attitude towards life and the world. Thus the protagonist of 'Garçon, un bock!' (Waiter, a Beer!), who has become a drunken, despondent layabout after witnessing a violent quarrel between his parents at the age of thirteen, is taken as expressing the author's adolescent trauma after his own parents' separation, despite the obvious dissimilarities between this self-destructive character and his creator (such as Maupassant's prodigious energy and vitality).[1] Perhaps the most striking example of such reductive interpretations is Pierre Cogny's study *Maupassant l'homme sans Dieu* (1968), the title of which (*Man Without God*) encapsulates its curious argument: since the atheistic Maupassant rejects Catholic orthodoxy in favour of Schopenhauerian pessimism, he is trapped in a 'blind alley', blocking any metaphysical solution to his despair and pity at man's destiny.[2] At no point does Cogny acknowledge that Maupassant rejects conventional religion and belief systems as a form of mystification designed to console and subordinate the weak and credulous, or recognize the paradox that, had Maupassant shared their credulity and conformism, he would have become a completely different writer.

A more balanced assessment of Maupassant's world view needs to disentangle the contradictions and paradoxes that his work reveals. French critic Mariane Bury argues that they arise

> from his ironic awareness of the instability of all forms of definitions and frontiers, in the domains of both knowledge and morality. In Maupassant's work, the madman is sane, the prostitute a saint, the criminal innocent, the mother a monster, the soldier sentimental, the man in the street a hero, the ridiculous old maid a romantic heroine, while at the same time, they are none of these.

In other words, the social categories into which people are inserted may accurately reflect their status, but negate or at least reveal little about their true character or temperament. To these ambivalent figures, one could add the writer's oscillation between cruelty and compassion (deploring mistreatment of animals, but celebrating hunting), and his apparently contradictory expressions of revulsion for literary production and journalism and meticulous dedication to artistic creation. Such twists and turns exemplify the ironist's sceptical refusal of simple, partial judgements and solutions. As Bury observes, 'stimulating questions rather than telling lies, such is the aim of ironic writing, a posture which presupposes that the ironist is not a cynic but a sincere conscience'.[3]

While the word irony was used pejoratively by Plato with the sense of dissemblance or feigning naivety, for Roman rhetoricians it acquired its familiar usage as a figure of discourse whose real meaning is contrary to what is overtly stated; by the nineteenth century it could apply equally to events and situations whose outcome contradicted expectations, and by extension to a mode of perception, a way of viewing existence, which stressed its absurdity, the incongruity between appearance and reality.[4] Its oblique nature is likely to deceive and irritate those who prefer plain speaking or writing to mocking evasion and ellipsis. In Maupassant's case, however, irony means more than simply debunking misguided characters or mocking naive readers; essentially it is a means of asserting positive values in the face of the crushing, tragic nature of existence. Such values include clear-sightedness, compassion, generosity and joy; typically, they allow characters or the narrator to escape the entrapment of the self by achieving moments of transcendence, in communion with others, nature or art. Perhaps the most striking irony revealed by his work is that he is not the misanthropic hack writer scorned by rivals and high-minded critics, but a frustrated idealist whose understated craftsmanship overrides his pessimism, at least for readers willing and able to appreciate his artistry.

Like many French writers of the post-romantic period and his *fin-de-siècle* generation (such as Flaubert and Gautier, or Huysmans, Rimbaud and Mallarmé), Maupassant's social and existential pessimism is partly counteracted by a compensatory belief in literary and artistic creation.[5] This is never developed into a coherent philosophical position; although he explicitly cites influential thinkers like Schopenhauer and Herbert Spencer, he makes no attempt to explicate their work, some of which he read in French translation. Offering a brief outline of their thought certainly illuminates Maupassant's pessimism and what some critics consider to be his Social Darwinism. His perception of humanity, civilization, nature, religion and artistic creativity is revealed most clearly by studying a small number of characteristic stories in the light of this broader cultural context.

We have already discussed how Maupassant quotes authorities like Schopenhauer and Spencer in 'La Lysistrata moderne' (1880) as a pretext for retailing the supposedly inherent intellectual defects of women; elsewhere he cites the psychiatrist Charcot's notorious exhibition of hysterical patients to justify the mocking assertion that hysteria has become a ubiquitous phenomenon

Ludwig Sigismund
Ruhl, *Arthur
Schopenhauer*, 1815,
oil on canvas.

('Une Femme', 1882).[6] From Maupassant's journalistic viewpoint,
the validity of their ideas is evidently less important than their
impact and notoriety, which he acknowledges with a certain
suspicion. Schopenhauer himself actually features in a brief story
called 'Auprès d'un mort', where he is introduced as 'the greatest
destroyer of dreams who ever passed through the world', yet
treated with curious irreverence.[7] A tubercular German recalls
how he spent the night following Schopenhauer's death watching
over his malodorous corpse, and was increasingly perturbed by
the Mephistophelian philosopher's grinning mouth. But this
posthumous expression of derision proves to be caused by his
protruding false teeth which finally fall on to the floor. Even the
most powerful thinker is thus unable to escape the humiliating
exigencies of mortality and physiology.[8]

Schopenhauer as an old man, photographed by Johann Schäfer in 1859.

Herbert Spencer (1820–1903), portrait by an unknown photographer in 1893.

Although Schopenhauer's major exposition of his philosophical system, *The World as Will and Representation*, was published in 1818, his work was largely ignored until the 1850s and reached an international audience only in the decades after his death in 1860. In France, Jean Bourdeau's anthology of his *Pensées, maximes et fragments* (1880) was read enthusiastically by intellectuals and writers, including Maupassant (who was a friend of the translator). The ennui, world-weariness and alienation so characteristic of the *fin-de-siècle* aesthete were apparently legitimized by Schopenhauer's trenchant aphorisms, in which one easily recognizes some of Maupassant's own views. His unflattering views of women as stunted, childish creatures have already been mentioned. He also anticipates Maupassant's opinion that 'the task of the novelist is not to narrate great events but to make small ones interesting,' while observing that 'he who writes for fools always finds a large public.'[9] It is less obvious that Maupassant had any real understanding of Schopenhauer's metaphysics.

For Schopenhauer, man is a metaphysical animal, and the world has a physical and an ethical existence. However, our civilized world 'is nothing but a great masquerade', driven largely by conflict and self-interest.[10] Christianity wrongly sunders men from the animal world and licenses the worst abuses of other creatures: 'Men are the devils of the earth, and the animals are the tormented souls.'[11] Yet human existence is worse: 'If the immediate and direct purpose of our life is not suffering, then our existence is the most ill-adapted to its purpose in the world.'[12] Suffering essentially derives from humans' greater capacity for knowledge: the Old Testament story of the Fall is 'the sole metaphysical truth' in that book, 'for our existence resembles nothing so much as the consequence of a misdeed, punishment for a forbidden desire'.[13] Schopenhauer rejects the Christian notion of a benevolent God and providential design, or for that matter the Hegelian conception of history as progressing towards a higher purpose.

Schopenhauer asserts that the empirical world of individuals and material phenomena which appear to work objectively through time, space and the causal relationships measured by science is actually created by human reason and senses (what he calls *Vorstellung*, usually translated as representation or idea). This physical world conceals a deeper metaphysical reality: what Plato called ideas and Kant the thing in itself, Schopenhauer calls will. The inner world of subjective individual consciousness and the unconscious belongs to will, a cosmic life force from which it has been detached: this fragmentation is a source of conflict and evil. He calls individual will 'the principle of bondage' and consciousness 'as it were a lightning flash momentarily illuminating the night'.[14] The demands of the will (whose phenomenal form is the body) are inseparable from individual suffering. Man can however achieve detachment from individual impulses and desires, through altruism or asceticism, or contemplation of universal ideas. These include artistic beauty: 'in the beautiful we always perceive the intrinsic and primary forces of animate and inanimate nature, that is to say Plato's Ideas thereof', which he calls a 'will-less subject of knowledge'.[15] Without will, there is no suffering: perception of the beautiful therefore (temporarily) abolishes suffering.

Schopenhauer does offer ethical and aesthetic solutions to humankind's apparently wretched lot. These resonated with *fin-de-siècle* writers like Huysmans, although their application may be questionable: his aesthetic dandy des Esseintes in *A rebours* supposedly rejects nature (which might be equated with the will to live), but in practice he fails to escape the demands of the body and indulges in all the sensual and material benefits enjoyed by the wealthy.[16] Similarly, while Marie-Claire Bancquart sees the existential nausea of the beer-drinking protagonist of 'Garçon, un bock!' as a form of lucidity, his egotistical, alcoholic depression hardly demonstrates abnegation and enlightenment.[17] A later story like 'L'Inutile Beauté' does however offer a more interesting reflection of or response to Schopenhauer. Before returning to this and other texts, a brief discussion of Darwin and Spencer is also helpful.

There is no evidence that Maupassant ever read Darwin (whose work was translated into French from the 1860s and certainly known to Zola), but he absorbed a version of Darwin's ideas indirectly through Herbert Spencer's application of evolutionary ideas to human society, usually known as Social Darwinism. Spencer was one of the founders of sociology in the mid-nineteenth century, his main preoccupation being power in society and the domination of individuals by collective forces. His key innovation 'was to apply the concept of natural selection to the problem of survival of groups', adumbrating an extreme laissez-faire ideology which found great favour in Victorian England, for it

> allayed the qualms of the rich about not helping the
> poor by telling them that the latter's sufferings were
> an inevitable price of progress which could occur only
> through the struggle for existence ending in the survival
> of the fittest and the elimination of the unfit.[18]

Although Spencer was regarded by his contemporaries as a progressive thinker for his fundamentalist liberalism, his arguments are now considered fallacious (anthropologists prefer to stress altruism, cooperation and husbanding of natural resources as key factors in the survival of social groups). Maupassant certainly shows human society to be ruthlessly competitive and regards inequality as an intrinsic part of human nature; he generally expresses little sympathy for social reformers, whose naive attempts to remedy injustice defy the laws of nature and the universe (hence the cruel derision expressed towards feminist campaigners in the early story 'Les Dimanches d'un bourgeois de Paris'). However, he also respects dominant, competitive individuals who succeed by defying social norms, and those who show compassion, generosity and remorse towards the victims and outcasts of society.

To sum up this discussion so far, Maupassant is an ironist in his sceptical detachment from routine human and social preoccupations (love, marriage, career, politics and so on), in his refusal of overt commitment to any cause other than literary art (and this too he sometimes questions). Like most writers of realist fiction, he is primarily interested in portraying specific individuals in small social groups; many of them seem destined to lead unhappy lives, by the very nature of human desire, mortality and social conflict. His inherent pessimism is further justified by the apparently bleak findings of Schopenhauer and Darwin: the individual counts for virtually nothing in terms of the evolution of the species or as a fragment of the will. However, the equivocal nature of his attitudes is suggested by his sociability and patent fascination with social groups and human behaviour; but the writer is a conscious observer rather than unthinking participant.

Characteristically, in 1876 he refused an invitation to join the Freemasons, on the grounds that 'I prefer to pay my boot maker rather than to be his equal,' and that 'I never wish to be linked to any political party of any kind, to any religion, to any sect, to any school.' He did however join the Société des gens de lettres, presumably for reasons of professional self-interest. Though already cited, his notorious comment in 1881 to Gisèle d'Estoc, that 'I place love within the religions, and religions within the greatest follies into which humanity has ever fallen', demands further clarification.[19] Conventional expressions of love and religious belief are mystifying *bêtises*, in that they are simply trite commonplaces, which bear little examination and patently fail to express or satisfy the true nature of physical desire and metaphysical anguish. But the underlying needs which they betray recur obsessively throughout Maupassant's work: to escape the confines of the self and mortality by intense communion with something beyond the individual, whether it is another person or group, the natural world, artistic creation, or a transcendent creative force.

The rest of this chapter returns to some of Maupassant's most imaginative and affecting stories, where such fundamental philosophical questions are skilfully embodied in memorable characters and dramatically situated in recognizable personal and social dilemmas. The short story (with its proximity to archetypal forms like myth and fable) arguably discloses the universal within the particular more effectively than the novel (Schopenhauer's recommendation that novels should concentrate on small events reflects his distrust of the genre). 'L'Inutile Beauté' (1890) is explicitly presented as a philosophical parable. This pleased Maupassant, though some critics and readers may find it unduly programmatic or lacking in coherence.[20]

In the opening section, the comtesse de Mascaret, a woman of great beauty and elegance, finally defies her violently jealous husband, who has fathered seven children with her in eleven years, with the deliberate but unsuccessful intention of disfiguring her so that she becomes undesirable to other men. Having been married against her will, she has lived the 'existence of a brood mare confined to a stud farm', and refuses to bear further offspring.[21] To avenge herself against his reproductive tyranny, she swears on oath that one of the children is not his. In the second section, we learn that, despite their mutual hatred, both count and countess love their many children; but unable to bear the uncertainty of not knowing which child is illegitimate, the count abandons wife and family and becomes a philandering *viveur*. In the third section, there is an odd shift in perspective: six years later, two men of the world discuss the implications of the countess's case in a philosophical dialogue reminiscent of Enlightenment thinkers like

Diderot and Sade. Finally, in an epilogue, the countess takes pity on her distressed husband and admits she was never unfaithful; she has gained her freedom and become the dominant partner.

The title 'L'Inutile Beauté' poses a question to which the story does not offer a straightforward answer. In what sense is women's beauty useless, unnecessary or superfluous? Schopenhauer remarks sourly that only sexual desire, the irresistible reproductive drive, makes stunted creatures like women seem beautiful to men.[22] But the story rejects such utilitarian determinism: the countess's beauty is biologically useless, since it is conserved by renouncing reproduction or even any sexual activity. This is further emphasized by the description of how she appears to the entranced gaze of the two philosophizing *mondains*: 'her pale complexion, gleaming like ivory, gave her the appearance of a statue, while in her hair that was black as night, a slender diadem curved like a rainbow, scattered with diamonds, shone like the milky way.'[23] In other words, she has transformed herself into a work of art, resembling a goddess more than a human being. By escaping the 'abominable law of reproduction that makes normal women into machines simply spawning beings', and natural instincts that reduce us to animals, she has achieved a 'poetic ideal'.[24] Rejection of human procreation leads the would-be philosophers to a wider rejection of God the creator, or rather a mindless will-to-live, endlessly spawning and destroying billions of creatures. Human intelligence is an accidental by-product of this endless fecundity. It makes humans aware how unfit they are for this world (only those debased to an animal state find it satisfying); but intelligence does allow the creation of civilization, which provides not merely material benefits but ideals like art and beauty. Even the brutish count finally becomes aware that his wife embodies 'a mystical beauty' which arouses 'immaterial appetites'.[25]

Though intriguing and thought-provoking, 'L'Inutile Beauté' raises objections both as a work of fiction and a philosophical tale.

Maupassant disregards his own criticism of didactic fiction, where characters are little more than vehicles for ideas or allegorical figures (the jealous husband, the beautiful wife, the provocative philosopher). His separation of civilization from nature, his conception of God, his attempt to combine materialism and idealism, all seem unpersuasive or incoherent. For example, many of the ills afflicting humanity that Maupassant depicts so graphically derive not from nature but from civilization: the enslavement of women in marriage, the impoverishment and corruption caused by unregulated capitalism, industrialized warfare, not to mention epidemics, famines, inequality and oppression. If human intelligence is seen as a product of an evolutionary process which favours the most efficient adaptation to an environment, then it makes more sense to argue that culture is part of nature, or that humanity has domesticated nature. In practice, few if any of his characters ever reject nature; indeed, he asserts in an article called 'L'Exil' that 'we are sons of the earth', formed by our native soil.[26] Similarly, if God is reduced to an immanent life force that drives natural laws, it seems odd to ascribe anthropomorphic qualities like incompetence or malevolence to what is effectively a material phenomenon like geology or biochemistry. And yet the celebration of beauty implies the existence of a transcendent realm that Maupassant is unable to conceptualize.

It is tempting to speculate that, had Maupassant known of his contemporary Nietzsche, he might well have embraced the latter's outright rejection of God, traditional metaphysics and morality, and celebration of Dionysian vitality and the superman's will to power.[27] As it is, his more fully developed characters often hold beliefs or commit acts that the author regards as misguided or wrong; but his imaginative empathy and avoidance of intrusive commentary forbid overt derision or condemnation. Far from dismissing religious beliefs, he is often prepared to present them seriously, especially when they are sincerely held by ordinary people. This is demonstrated in his well-known early story 'La Maison Tellier', a model of joyous comic virtuosity. This tale gave its title to the writer's first collection of stories, published by Victor Havard in May 1881. Although the bawdy subject matter caused the book to be banned from sale in Hachette's railway bookshops (to Maupassant's annoyance), his frankness was rapidly accepted by the press and most readers. Louis Forestier notes in particular the author's provocative juxtaposition of sacred and profane in 'La Maison Tellier' and what he calls a 'sacrilegious' representation of a Catholic mass.[28]

'La Maison Tellier' (translated as 'Madame Tellier's establishment' by H.N.P. Sloman) is a house of prostitution in the coastal town of Fécamp.[29] Several of Maupassant's contemporaries had already broached this taboo area, in rather puritanical, long-winded novels which uneasily combine bourgeois prurience with sententious emphasis on vice and degradation.[30] In comparison, Maupassant's approach is crisply refreshing: in less than 10,000 words, he presents the brothel as an established and necessary social institution, which services the needs of the flesh much like the Church serves the needs of the spirit. Twenty-first-century readers may find this unabashed defence of the sex industry more shocking than the comparison with organized religion. In fact the whole story mischievously develops a parallel between the two institutions; while the first provides release from sexual desire and social constraints, the second allows spiritual release and communion with the divine. Both therefore offer experiences that break the restraints and monotony of everyday existence. Hence the opening sentence: 'on allait là, chaque soir, vers onze heures, comme au café, simplement.'[31] Sloman translates this as: 'you went there every evening about eleven o'clock, quite naturally, as if it had been a public-house.'[32] 'You' seems to include the reader as a potential visitor, whereas the following pages actually show that

Vincent van Gogh, *The Brothel* (*Le Lupanar*), 1888, oil on canvas.

the house is rather more selective and replicates the hierarchy and divisions of provincial life. For example, the clients are exclusively male, and the employees entirely female, apart from a muscular barman. The well-furnished, upstairs rooms are reserved for prosperous middle-class businessmen and officials, whereas the shabby ground-floor bar is frequented by rowdy working men and sailors. The widowed Madame Tellier has inherited the house and runs it like a respectable business, much like a pub or girls' school; she insists on being treated accordingly. Not only are her employees compared to schoolgirls or cloistered nuns (when they enjoy country outings), but the lantern lighting the house entrance resembles those placed below Madonnas set in town walls.[33]

One evening, however, the lantern is extinguished and the establishment closed, to the consternation of the regular clients and rage of the sailors: Madame Tellier has taken the entire female household to attend the first communion of her niece in a village

Henri de Toulouse-Lautrec, *First Communion Day*, 1888, grisaille on cardboard.

60 miles away. A commercial traveller on the train asks humorously if they are moving to a new convent, and then gives them free garters (fitting each one personally). But the more naive peasants in the village fail to recognize their provenance: as the girls arrive in their gaudy finery, a half-blind old woman mistakes them for a religious procession. Their appearance in the church dazzles both the congregation and officiating priest. All are overcome by emotion as the 'ineffable mystery' of the communion proceeds and they feel the presence of 'something superhuman, an all-pervading soul, the prodigious breath of an invisible, almighty being'. For the priest, this is nothing short of 'a true, great, sublime miracle', which they owe to the presence of Madame Tellier's pious sisters.[34]

Maupassant takes care to describe the ceremony without a hint of mockery: the women's piety and emotion are genuinely felt and the priest's interpretation plausible and orthodox (though unlikely if he had realized their true occupation). Though neither the author nor many readers may feel the need to believe in miracles or Catholic dogma, he is not satirizing religious faith or peasants' gullibility; from a purely humanist viewpoint, the ritual and ceremony are still genuinely moving in their affirmation of a collective, transcendental experience, even if it actually derives from the power of the collective imagination rather than the supernatural. The household soon reverts to its more customary antics. Madame is enraged on finding her drunken brother trying to ravish one of the girls. But this troubling juxtaposition or confusion of sacred and profane heightens the story's impact. When the brothel re-opens after the flock's return, they enjoy a more secular, sensual celebration, Madame even reducing the price of champagne by 40 per cent to 6 francs a bottle, on the grounds that *ça n'est pas tous les jours fête* (holidays don't come every day).[35] At the very least, the *fête* temporarily liberates the girls and their clients from their servitude; perhaps the holiday is even a holy day, allowing a return to childhood innocence and purity.

'La Maison Tellier' skilfully modulates these shifts between bawdy comedy and moments of pathos, maintaining an ironical detachment that does not prevent the reader from being moved by the characters' emotions, if not their piety. Maupassant's shorter stories about religious belief are often weakened by more overt derision. Thus in 'La Relique' (1882), a doctor offers his pious fiancée a fake religious relic. To convince her of its authenticity, he assures her he stole it from Cologne cathedral; she is delighted by this sacrilegious display of devotion. When his lie is revealed, however, she threatens to break off their engagement, unless he acquires a genuine relic certified by the Holy Father in person. An irreligious joke backfires similarly in 'Mon oncle Sosthène' (1882). Here a nephew mischievously sends a Jesuit priest to visit his uncle, an anti-clerical Freemason who mistakenly believes he is dying; but far from expelling the priest, the gullible uncle is converted by him and disinherits the impious nephew. Sceptics should note however that, in each story, the disbelieving pranksters come off worse than those whose naive faith is the ostensible object of mockery.

A more substantial novella, 'Miss Harriet' (1884), also reverses the initial configuration of plot and characters, but in a subtler fashion. Crude derision of religious credulity or foolish jesting is replaced by a tragicomic depiction of those who seem fated to be at odds with the universe. The painter Léon Chenal recalls his youthful, carefree wandering along the Norman coast, the sensual and artistic delights experienced by such 'honeymoons with the earth'.[36] In one village, he encounters Miss Harriet, an elderly spinster, who seems at first sight to be a grotesque mummy, a typically repressed and puritanical eccentric Englishwoman. The two characters appear to be exact opposites. The painter is a seductive, articulate Frenchman, a creative spirit at ease with himself and the world; the old maid is compared to a scarecrow, a repellent, unbalanced figure whose maladroit foreignness immediately arouses scorn and dislike in the local community.

ŒUVRES COMPLÈTES ILLUSTRÉES

DE

GUY DE MAUPASSANT

MISS
HARRIET

Illustrations de CH. MOREL

Gravure sur bois
de G. LEMOINE

PARIS

Société d'Éditions Littéraires et Artistiques

LIBRAIRIE PAUL OLLENDORFF

50, CHAUSSÉE D'ANTIN, 50

Edition of *Miss Harriet* (1901), with illustrations by Charles Morel.

Yet they are gradually revealed to be kindred spirits, whose sensitivity to artistic and natural beauty separates both of them from the utilitarian concerns of the local community. Thus while the peasants are outraged by her misplaced kindness to animals which they regard as vermin or prey, the painter is touched by her appreciation of his painting and her pantheistic ecstasy at the sight of a magnificent sunset. Their budding friendship, however, is cut short by her dismay when she discovers him flirting with the maid. Overwhelmed by her frustrated affection, Miss Harriet disappears into the night, and the next day her body is found in the well, a victim of what the painter calls 'the eternal injustice of implacable nature', which denied her love but reclaims her body for its generation of new life.[37]

The painter doubts that Miss Harriet will find the compensation she hoped for in an afterlife: her soul has been extinguished at the bottom of the well (like that of the suicidal protagonist of *Fort comme la mort*). As already noted, Catholic critics are dissatisfied with such affirmations of a materialistic pantheism; while Pierre Cogny saw Maupassant as trapped in a 'blind alley', his contemporary Paul Bourget called him a 'nihilist hungering for the absolute'.[38] In fact, he shows little sympathy for nihilists or those who reject ordinary humane values: witness the portrayal of child-murderers in 'La Petite Roque' and 'Moiron' as deluded maniacs. Unlike Schopenhauer, Maupassant refuses to contemplate the metaphysical as anything other than a nebulous hypothesis. He has no desire to be a prophet or a philosopher. But his pessimistic detachment and scepticism do not prevent his writing from conveying ethical and aesthetic values, the most important of which is the creative power of the literary imagination in its construction of a richly detailed, autonomous fictional world. In *Qu'est-ce que la littérature?*, Sartre asserts that behind the aesthetic imperative there is always a moral one: 'the work of art . . . is an act of confidence in the freedom of men'; the act of writing is itself an assertion of freedom.[39]

Readers may be saddened by the account of a foolish old woman who commits suicide when happiness is within her reach, but a story like 'Miss Harriet' is actually memorable and pleasurable because it communicates a whole range of human experience in a way that is celebratory and life-embracing. Mariane Bury argues persuasively that Maupassant practises what she calls a poetics of the real; that is, he 'accepts the limits of pessimism to exalt the evident, sensual and sublime presence of things as they are'.[40] Within a literary text, a work of the imagination, pessimistic awareness of the human condition and the limitations of our senses do not necessarily impede harmonious integration with the world.

Indeed the senses are the key to Maupassant's art, for they connect his characters and narrators to the natural and social world, effacing the suffering and isolation brought by individual consciousness and thought. Hence the insistence on sight, smell, hearing and touch in the innumerable brief descriptive passages and figurative turns of phrase that evoke the material context and transient moments of fulfilment experienced throughout his fictional works and travelogues. To conclude with a brief illustrative example, in the story 'Une partie de campagne' (A Day in the Country), the lovers' amorous encounter is partly triggered by the naive Henriette's desire to hear the song of a nightingale. Although this is at first gently mocked as a romantic cliché, an erotic parallel is then developed over a page as the girl's ecstasy is matched by the rising and falling of the bird's exuberant song:

The bird became intoxicated, and its voice, gradually accelerating like a fire spreading or passion swelling, seemed to be accompanying the crackling of kisses beneath the tree. Then its delirious song was released in frenzy, with long, swooning single notes and shuddering spasms of melody. At times, it rested briefly, uttering only one or two quiet sounds, which climaxed suddenly in a shrill note.[41]

Although Louis Forestier suggests that such transitory moments of bliss can only blight the characters' routine existence, the story concludes more hopefully with the implied promise of future encounters. And readers can enter the liberating world of fiction whenever they desire.

7

Afterlives

Maupassant wrote a great deal, had a colourful sex life and died miserably as a result. Unlike other famous French writers of his age (such as political campaigners like Victor Hugo and Émile Zola), he never entered the public sphere except as a journalist. In other words, Maupassant's life and career interest us mainly because he was a talented and original writer whose posthumous appeal has extended to an ever widening audience. It therefore seems appropriate to conclude this study by examining not only his enduring literary influence, but his broader cultural legacy, in particular the changing production, adaptation and reception of his work over the 127 years since his death. For his contemporaries, Maupassant was a popular storyteller, journalist and wealthy socialite whose success was tragically cut short by illness and insanity. While his premature decline and demise aroused a rather morbid fascination in the press and literary world, their true causes and pathology were only understood and acknowledged in the second half of the twentieth century, when more reliable biographies and complete editions of his correspondence became available.

There was a similar time lag in the establishment of his literary reputation as a classic author: until the 1950s, many highbrow critics and writers regarded his accessibility and clarity as negative evidence, justifying a facile assumption that Maupassant's talent was primarily commercial and therefore trivial and ephemeral.

Maupassant's tomb in Montparnasse cemetery, Paris.

Hence the negative assessments by Paul Morand and Edmond de Goncourt (cited in previous chapters), or the dismissive judgements cited in the surveys conducted by the Franco-American academic Artine Artinian in the mid-twentieth century.[1] Between 1938 and 1955, Artinian invited 147 well-known European and American writers to comment briefly on Maupassant's status and influence. These were supposedly the decades marking his eclipse, when he was perceived somewhat condescendingly as a *conteur populaire* fit for schoolchildren and semi-educated readers, but of little interest to serious intellectuals and innovative artists. Several French writers (for instance, Georges Duhamel and André Gide) concede that Maupassant is esteemed more highly elsewhere (in the u.s., uk, Russia and Germany), but despite (or perhaps because of) this international allure they relegate him to a lowly status as a talented craftsman. On the other hand, while authors who occupy an avant-garde position in their respective fields, such as the poet Valéry, the dramatist Claudel and the novelist Céline, predictably dismiss his work as uninteresting and outdated, writers like Thomas Mann and John Buchan who themselves are internationally recognized authors of socially realistic novels and stories readily acknowledge Maupassant's universality. But if Maupassant's belated readmission in the second half of the twentieth century to the canon of original, influential authors reflects the acceptance of short realistic narrative as a significant literary form, it also illustrates the democratization and commercialization of culture. Recognizing someone as a classic author involves not merely reaffirming the originality and prestige of his or her work but appropriating it for new purposes.

As we have seen, somewhat ironically, Maupassant himself was equally dismissive of popular writers like Dumas, Sue and Sand whom he considered to lack the artistry which could be appreciated only by an elite group of discerning readers. He himself had no aspiration to become a writer aiming at a mass audience. Indeed, during his lifetime, Maupassant's readership was largely restricted to a relatively small group of privileged readers able to afford the high prices charged by publishers of novels and literary reviews. In December 1891, he estimated total sales of his books over the previous twelve years to be 373,000 copies, or about 15,000 per volume of work; while pre-publication of stories and novels in newspapers and reviews was as lucrative as sales of books, as he wryly observed, it also reduced the number of potential buyers of expensive volumes.[2] In other words, one can estimate from these figures that, although his books sold extremely well by the standards of the age (when sales of 3,000 copies of a novel were considered respectable), the average number of readers of most of Maupassant's books in the 1880s is unlikely to have exceeded 100,000 people. A readership which seems surprisingly modest from a twenty-first-century perspective – used to book sales counted in millions – nonetheless gave him prestige and a very comfortable income. That said, the short-lived Maupassant was far from being the most commercially successful French author of the late nineteenth century. For example, Zola sold about 2.6 million books, Alphonse Daudet 2.2 million, and less well-known writers like Georges Ohnet and Paul Bourget over 1 million each.[3]

Most writers who enjoy high sales and popularity at some point during their lifetime are rapidly forgotten as their output declines and they are supplanted by rivals in a highly competitive literary market. Thus successful novelists like Bourget and Ohnet soon lost their large readership and became practically unknown to later generations of readers, demoted to the ranks of minor writers read only by scholars and aficionados.[4] On the other hand, a possible quantitative definition of an author who has attained classic status would be one who continues to attract significant numbers of readers across the world in the decades and centuries after his or her death. Maupassant clearly falls into this category; in fact, he became a writer with a truly international mass audience only

Bust of Maupassant made in 1897 by Raoul Verlet, in the Parc Monceau, Paris.

in the twentieth century. Although it is virtually impossible to obtain accurate sales information about authors whose works are outside copyright, the global proliferation since the last century of thousands of translations and editions of his works suggests *annual* sales of his books now far exceed Maupassant's cumulative figure of 373,000 for his entire career. There are for example literally hundreds of editions of his individual works and story collections currently available in French, many of them aimed at the school market, where he is a perennial figure.

No doubt Maupassant would have been pleased by his enduring, posthumous celebrity and by his international recognition as a writer whose works encapsulate the spirit of *fin-de-siècle* France and whose limpid artistry still moves readers across the world. On the other hand, given his aesthetic and social elitism, what would he have made of the adaptation and transformation of his work to fit school texts and curricula or the demands of new media like cinema, television and comic books? Perhaps such speculations seem otiose. The key point is that Maupassant is no longer simply a deceased author of lasting aesthetic appeal as a compelling storyteller and limpid stylist: he has also become a brand name, a cultural and commercial icon used to promote the manifold manifestations and manipulations of the heritage industry (like many other artists and writers, such as Jane Austen and the Brontës in the UK). Some of these avatars are predictable and have relatively innocuous aims, such as attracting tourists to sites in Normandy associated with Maupassant, or the study of his texts by learned societies and Internet discussion groups. But some of the more significant transformations of high culture into mass culture merit fuller investigation: what remains of the author when his texts are reconfigured for purposes beyond his original intention or conception?

At a basic level, this may simply involve redistributing his stories in new ways that emphasize the range of his inventiveness.[5] Thus Maupassant's frequent appearance in anthologies devoted to horror, the fantastic or science fiction confirms that his appeal extends beyond the social realism and the documenting of everyday life which are usually assumed to be his key characteristics.[6] On the other hand, while his attractiveness to younger readers may seem equally positive and to justify pedagogic exploitation, its consequences are not always beneficial. As was already noted, most readers of Maupassant probably first encounter his works either in editions aimed at schoolchildren and students or in translated anthologies. No doubt such publications have the laudable aim of introducing a dramatic storyteller, an accessible exponent of nineteenth-century French culture, to an uninformed but potentially receptive audience. Inevitably, however, commercial viability, the target audience and pedagogic utility demand certain compromises in the selection and annotation of texts. One assumes, for example, that a version of *Contes et nouvelles* that turns out to be a 24-page 'BD en français facile adaptée par Colette Samson' (comic book in easy French, with accompanying CD and activities, Paris, 2013) is aimed at very young children. But the temptation to edulcorate, truncate or otherwise censor Maupassant is one which many editors of such collections have failed to resist, even when their intended audience is considerably older. While most do this surreptitiously, by simply omitting his more provocative and disturbing stories, a minority unscrupulously abridge texts they consider unseemly or simply too long.[7] The consequence is that the Maupassant of school editions is a much blander writer than the author of 'Les Soeurs Rondoli', 'La Petite Roque', 'L'Inconnue' and other adult stories which readers will only find in complete editions. One suspects that many people who have dismissed Maupassant as a facile, immature yarn-spinner have limited their acquaintance with his works to reading such emasculated textbooks.

Similarly, although the proliferation of translations of his works into most Western and many other languages is welcome evidence of Maupassant's universality, the quality of some translations sometimes leaves much to be desired. Insofar as translation is a form of adaptation of a written text (transferring it from one linguistic and cultural setting into another), it poses technical and ethical problems much like those confronted by anyone adapting a story or novel for another medium (such as film or theatre). Thus, until the later twentieth century, the sexually frank nature of Maupassant's work posed problems both for his translators and writers and directors of film and stage versions. In the prudish climate of late Victorian England, translations of Maupassant (and

Zola) were heavily censored (although the pioneering translator and publisher Henry Vizetelly still suffered prosecution and imprisonment for his endeavours). Expurgation was frequently the case in the USA, where the lack of international enforcement of copyright also meant that his work was shamelessly plagiarized. Around the turn of the twentieth century, pirated translations of Maupassant also included dozens of 'Americanizations' that bore no resemblance to anything he had written.[8]

That said, reputable translation evidently requires a fidelity to the original text which may be impossible or undesirable in adaptations to other media. It may not occur to monolingual readers that translation is a problematic art; a good or bad translation can either stimulate or destroy one's appreciation of foreign writers, irrespective of the quality of their original texts. But anyone who has carefully compared even an accurate and fluent translation with the original will invariably have discovered errors, omissions and stylistic and cultural infelicities. This is why I have normally avoided using published translations into English when citing Maupassant's texts in this book; even the most authoritative translations tend to deviate from the syntax and lexis or cultural markers of the French text, foregrounding readability and accessibility and eliminating idiosyncrasies or obscurities that obstruct legibility. For all his clarity, Maupassant challenges even skilled professional translators (particularly in finding effective equivalents for dialect, cultural concepts, synonyms expressing emotions, characteristic rhythms and turns of phrase).[9]

It is not my intention to distribute praise or blame to particular translators (or editors of anthologies), or to offer specific examples of successes and failings at this late stage. From a more pragmatic viewpoint, the twenty-first-century reader of Maupassant has access in French via Kindle apps or the Internet to reliable electronic editions of most of his written work virtually free of charge; anyone studying the writer in depth would however be strongly advised to acquire recent editions edited by reputable scholars. Readers dependent on translations are in a more awkward position. As far as English translations are concerned, their quality ranges from excellent to deplorable. As a rule, when the translator is explicitly named on the title page and his or her expertise is summarized on the cover or inside the book, the reader can expect to be well served. Unfortunately, good up-to-date translations by experts are relatively expensive, whereas anonymous or amateurish translations that are outside copyright cost publishers nothing. Maupassant's purportedly complete works are available in English on Kindle for the price of a newspaper, but readers sensitive to style and fluency are likely to be disappointed by what they are offered.

Despite these reservations, the vast expansion of the literate public and electronic sources means that readers of Maupassant's texts in the twenty-first century can access and sample them in many languages, far more cheaply and easily than would have been imaginable in his age (or even the mid-twentieth century). Thirty-five years ago, to read his correspondence I had to travel to the Bibliothèque Nationale in Paris and spend days peering at a fuzzy microfiche copy of a printed edition long out of print; this material is now freely available online. Ironically, adaptations of individual works as films and BDS (*bandes dessinées* or graphic novels and stories) are now much more expensive than digitized editions of his complete works, or simply unobtainable. Like translation, adaptation of his work into other media began during his lifetime, with similarly mixed results. We have already discussed the sacrifices and expansions necessitated by theatre adaptations like *Mouche*. While translations may be expected to reflect the original text as accurately as the culture, syntax and semantics of another language permit, fidelity to the original written source is not usually considered a very useful criterion for understanding and appraising adaptations into media that are not text-based. They are much better judged in terms of the end-product's use of the techniques and conventions of the medium into which they are transferred, or the losses and gains brought by the shift from a written text to a visual and/or aural medium.[10]

For example, the writer and director of a BBC radio play called *The Inn* (originally broadcast in 2006 and again in 2018, written by Sue Glover), deriving from the story 'L'Auberge' about two men and a dog trapped over winter in a Swiss alpine inn, faced the challenge of converting Maupassant's lengthy descriptions of the beauty and terrors of the high mountains, and the surviving man's deteriorating physical and mental state after the disappearance of his companion, into plausible dialogue and sound effects.[11] In practice, since there is very little dialogue in the original story and the characters are minimally developed, all that remains of Maupassant in the radio play is his melodramatic plot along with the snoring dog and howling blizzards (and of course his name as a famous French author more likely to attract listeners than a relatively unknown Scottish adaptor). Much of the play in fact consists of two sombre monologues, first from a young woman who is barely mentioned in the original story, and then from the surviving guide left alone with the dog. The decision to insert a dominant female character (romantically attracted to the young guide) gives the play a new dynamic tension, and might be seen as a feminist riposte to Maupassant's tendency to downplay female characters. Another rather more lively BBC radio adaptation, of *The Hand* by Michael Robson (directed by Derek Hoddinott, first broadcast in 1976 and repeated in 2018), also substantially rewrites Maupassant's fantastical story about the vengeance inflicted on an eccentric Englishman by an amputated hand which he keeps as a macabre trophy. Much of the plot, dialogue and characters' interactions are entirely reinvented by the adaptor, so that the play becomes an entertaining pastiche of a late Victorian mystery in the style of H. Rider Haggard or Arthur Conan Doyle (except that, true to Maupassant, the mystery remains inexplicable).

Drama demands stylized spectacle (including soundscapes), dialogue, action and the embodiment of characters (if only as voices), whereas literary novels and stories may consist largely of descriptions and reflections presented by a single narrator. Stripping Maupassant's narrative voice from his stories also removes essential descriptive and psychological elements, without which their overdetermined plots and memorable characters tend towards the simplified melodrama and caricatural stereotypes of popular fiction and soap opera. This may be why I have never seen (or heard) a dramatized version of Maupassant that rose above the level of entertainment or impoverished imitation. On the other hand, I have seen inspiring stage productions of Zola's *Thérèse Raquin* (perhaps because this early novel is a lurid melodrama, much improved by the removal of Zola's didactic commentary). In any case, fiction is usually considered to be more compatible with film, which is primarily a visual, kinetic medium; Maupassant's naturalism and impressionistic, mobile descriptive passages have often been perceived as essentially cinematic, which may explain why his work has been relentlessly pillaged by the cinema and television industry for over a century.[12]

The reincarnation of Maupassant's work in feature films and televisual versions demonstrates at the very least the inspirational and timeless quality of his storytelling; the quality of the films is another matter. It is a truism to observe that great books make bad movies (and vice versa). Anyone who appreciates *War and Peace*'s epic grandeur and profundity probably finds the filmed versions deeply embarrassing, whereas *The Three Musketeers*' swashbuckling adventures come to life on film (or even in a comic book), when they are liberated from Dumas' wooden writing and perfunctory characterization. Maupassant's work is inherently filmable, in that it is naturalistic, relatively brief, and has the universal nature of fable. Unsurprisingly, there are more than a hundred film versions, some of them from renowned *auteurs* like Josef von Sternberg, John Ford, Jean Renoir, Max Ophüls, Luis Buñuel and Jean-Luc Godard.[13] Closer investigation however is not always encouraging. For example, Buñuel remarked of his *Una mujer sin amor* (A Woman Without Love, 1951), a remake of Cayatte's adaptation of *Pierre et Jean*, that it was 'quite simply the worst movie I ever made'.[14] Renoir's *Partie de campagne* (1946) was released in an unfinished version, and how much classics like *Shanghai Express*, *Stagecoach* and *Masculin-féminin* really owe to Maupassant is highly debatable.

Filmographies list multiple adaptations of over fifty stories and five novels (excluding *Notre coeur*). These include silent versions released from 1908 to 1927, two of them produced in Russia, and talkies produced outside France in Japan, Sweden, Finland, Italy, Germany, Argentina, the USA and the UK. There have also been innumerable adaptations made for French television and radio, as well as a BBC production scripted by Robert Muller of *Bel-Ami* in 1971. As well as plays and films about Maupassant himself, Eric Crozier's libretto of Benjamin Britten's comic opera *Albert Herring* (1947) derives from 'Le Rosier de Madame Husson'. In July 1979, Bernard Pivot's celebrated cultural chat show *Apostrophes* (which drew large French TV audiences unimaginable in most other countries) was devoted to Maupassant; the panel discussing the author included not only a well-known scholar, biographer and film-maker, but the then president of the republic, Valéry Giscard d'Estaing (himself a novelist and member of the Académie française, who modestly conceded his own writing was much inferior). Such a profusion of iterations certainly demonstrates Maupassant's undiminished cultural influence, which endures to the present day, with for example the release of feature films derived from *Bel-Ami* and *Une Vie* in 2012 and 2016.

Assessing the intrinsic quality of this material is less relevant to a discussion focused on Maupassant's survival and legacy as a writer than posing the question: how much of Maupassant actually survives in such cultural transformations? Given practical constraints, our answer has to be limited to examples derived from three works discussed in previous chapters, namely *Bel-Ami*, 'Le Horla', and 'La Maison Tellier'. Most of the directors and writers behind the many film adaptations of *Bel-Ami* are clearly aware of the novel's cultural status (indeed this is probably the key factor underwriting their production), reflected in high production values and lush recreation of the Belle Époque setting. The novel is enhanced cinematographically, in the sense it becomes a glamorous visual and aural spectacle, with charismatic actors in authentic costumes and settings that echo painters like Renoir and Toulouse-Lautrec. This of course is the positive side of heritage cinema. The treatment of the novel's psychological and satirical dimensions is more problematic.

Whereas the 1971 BBC TV adaptation was broadcast in five hour-long episodes, the novel's length, wealth of detail, plot complexities and profusion of characters all inevitably demand radical compression to fit a feature film or stage play viewed in a single session. Frédéric Dard's stage adaptation (performed in Paris in 1954) ruthlessly eliminates secondary characters and streamlines the plot, while drawing much of the dialogue from the novel and using a narrator to read out transitional passages.[15] There is little sense of time or place, and Bel-Ami becomes a villain of melodrama, a caricatural *arriviste*. While the pre-war German version, directed by Willi Forst in 1939, insists with a certain relish on the political and financial corruption of the protagonists (usually seen as reflecting Nazi anti-French propaganda), the 1955 version directed by Louis Daquin was initially banned in France because it accurately reflected the novel's hostile account of French colonialism (at a time when an undeclared civil war was breaking out in Algeria). Daquin and his screenwriters Vailland and Pozner were all members of the French communist party (which may have provided financial backing).[16] Hollywood morality, on the other hand, was unable to tolerate Duroy's unimpeded ascent by manipulating women and duping rivals. In Albert Lewin's *The Private Affairs of Bel-Ami* (1947), starring George Sanders, the overweening Duroy is finally eliminated in a duel with a rival.

The most recent film adaptation, a 2012 joint UK/French/Italian production shot in Budapest and London, and directed by Declan Donnellan and Nick Ormerod (better known as founders of the Cheek by Jowl theatre company), is unimpeded by the overt or tacit censorship of sexual intimacy or political controversy imposed on films in the 1940s and 1950s. Scripted by Rachel Bennette, it features Robert Pattinson (star of the *Twilight* franchise) as Duroy, with Uma Thurman as Madeleine, Christina Ricci as Clotilde, and Kristin Scott Thomas as Virginie Rousset. One wonders why the Walter family are renamed Rousset, which of course effaces their Jewish connections. Or why the film is set in 1890, five years after the novel was published. Despite their various nationalities, the cast all adopt British accents (although only Kristin Scott Thomas manages to pronounce French names correctly) and certainly look ravishing in period costumes. Given the odd conventions of international productions (whereby anglophones play francophones, or a French actress can play Lady Macbeth in English and a black American actor the African dictator Idi Amin), their performances are quite acceptable. In its representation of the diverse settings of *fin-de-siècle* Paris, from the gloom of sordid neighbourhoods, lodgings and bars to the resplendent luxury of wealthy bourgeois cafés and residences, the film is visually compelling in the way it illustrates Duroy's rising trajectory. The mirror scenes that capture his outward transformation from shabby clerk to elegant boulevardier are skilfully intercalated.

Critics were however less convinced by Robert Pattinson's metamorphosis from male model and cute vampire to leading actor in a serious historical film. Thus the *Washington Post* called his performance 'undead', while the *New York Times* said of the film as a whole, 'although this is potentially juicy stuff, it is as dry and tasteless as a shrunken piece of fruit left in the refrigerator for too long.'[17] Actually Pattinson looks youthful, suave and rakish, and meaningfully fondles Clo's neck in one scene; his slightly feminine manner and blood-sucking credentials correspond well to Duroy's role as a gigolo and parasite. In a particularly effective sequence, the dying Forestier (whose wife and career Duroy usurps) coughs blood over his erstwhile protégé; we cut directly to a shot of Duroy looking into his mentor's grave, which proves to be a premonitory dream. In a couple of relatively explicit sex scenes, we see Pattinson's naked buttocks heaving, rather than his partner's body; he breaks off writing an article with Madeleine for a bout of grunting copulation, which she impatiently hurries to a conclusion.

The film's real problems have little to do with its competent actors, excellent art direction and cinematography, but stem from the writer's and directors' struggle to contain the novel's plot and convey its satirical message within one hundred minutes. In consequence, Duroy emerges as a somewhat petulant and venal womanizer, rather than as an able journalist and political intriguer. While his overt antagonism towards his chiefs Forestier and Rousset (who attempt to fire him from the newspaper) and hasty seduction of Mme Rousset and her daughter may be justifiable in accelerating the plot and emphasizing adversarial relationships, such a change of tempo is accompanied by crudely melodramatic, moralizing confrontations between Duroy and the three women (whose attraction towards him seems barely explicable). The political and financial dimensions are curtailed so radically as to be virtually incomprehensible, and the disgrace of Laroche, divorce from Madeleine and elopement with Suzanne are despatched with such rapidity that the characters seem passionless and mechanical. While readers of *Bel-Ami* are likely to be disappointed by this crude simplification of the novel's psychological and social relationships, most other viewers probably dismiss this film as a picturesque but forgettable costume drama; it attracted only modest audiences on its theatrical release, earning just enough to recoup production costs.

Adaptations of Maupassant's stories create fewer problems, at least in the sense their plot and characters do not require such brutal compression. 'Le Horla' has been remade several times for stage and film, and is also currently available in an audio version and two French BDS. Although for twenty-first-century viewers, comic books tend to resemble the storyboard of a motion picture – in other words, a static, primitive version of a film – it is worth recalling that the telling of a narrative through a sequence of pictures (with or without an accompanying written text) long pre-dates the invention of cinema (or indeed the realistic novel and story). Thus historians of comics draw our attention not only to the Bayeux tapestry in the late eleventh century, but to Sumerian and Egyptian narrative pictograms dating back millennia. While illustrated editions of Maupassant's works were published during his lifetime, the establishment of the graphic novel or story as a popular form of narration in the mid-twentieth century subordinates written text to image. Abridged versions of classic novels and stories as comic books have been commonplace for nearly a century, although most are aimed at younger audiences.[18]

However, Guillaume Sorel's more sophisticated interpretation of 'Le Horla' as a BD (Paris, 2014) effectively resituates Maupassant's solipsistic narrator compiling his tormented diary of possession within the external, natural and social world of late nineteenth-century France. The album's 62 pages offer us, in five hundred colour panels, a series of still images that replace or reimagine the written text (many of them have no dialogue). Compared to the cartoonish and schematic style of most BDS, Sorel's artwork is meticulous and aesthetically appealing, at times intentionally copying painters like Degas and Toulouse-Lautrec. The spaces and places in which the protagonist exists are not merely background illustrations, but convey and contain threat and danger. One admires the muted colours and polished sheen of the parquet floor in the narrator's mansion, while noting its sombre isolation; the luxuriant woodland which surrounds it ends in plunging cliffs. A trapped bird struggles to escape through a window which it cannot comprehend (as the narrator struggles against his translucent foe). High-level perspectives reveal the house's position adjoining the river, along which the Brazilian three-master passes. The narrator is given a cat as a companion and witness. The cat flees for three days after the ship passes and the narrator's malaise and foreboding increase. In his nightmares, the Horla is depicted as a vaporous nude male figure, perhaps emerging from his body, crouching on his chest, draining his vital fluids. When the narrator leaves, his coachman suffers similar symptoms. After his return, the cat stops him falling or jumping off the cliff, and survives the final conflagration that destroys the house and servants, but not the protagonist and the Horla. The discursive metaphysical speculations that dominate the end of the story are presented more summarily, accompanied by images evoking the mysteries of the cosmos.

Readers may well feel that Sorel's replacement of these essayistic ruminations with visual equivalents is a gain rather than a loss. Max Ophüls's 1952 film of 'La Maison Tellier' also adds a pleasing visual, kinetic dimension to Maupassant's story (with a narrative voice-over somewhat redundantly citing the text), while retaining its blend of gaiety and pathos. This longer story is sandwiched between two briefer sketches ('Le Masque' and 'Le Modèle'), forming a disparate trilogy which is linked by the title *Le Plaisir* and an off-screen commentary supposedly from Maupassant. Ophüls and his screenwriter Jacques Natanson planned to use 'La Femme de Paul' as the third story, even constructing the set; but a new producer shied away from Maupassant's explicit treatment of lesbianism and demanded a blander replacement. As it is, the film's treatment of prostitution is more discreet than Maupassant's: the spectator is never allowed inside Mme Tellier's establishment, which we observe only through its outside windows as the camera moves horizontally and vertically along its walls. The comedy is also broader, yet more prudish (the clients' sexual activity is virtually unmentionable). While Madeleine Renaud endows Mme Tellier with forceful charm, Jean Gabin's drunken mugging as her lecherous brother becomes wearisome. After Maupassant's concluding line *ça n'est pas tous les jours fête* (it's not every day you get a holiday), we watch the party continuing through the window shutters and the narrator informs us we have seen a 'meeting of pleasure and purity'. This sentimental insistence on pleasure is more characteristic of Ophüls than Maupassant; his three stories are really about love, desire and the sacrifices and compromises which they entail rather than hedonistic celebration. And despite its undoubted visual charm and masterful cinematography, the compromises necessitated in filming Maupassant in the 1950s now make Ophüls' film look quaintly dated.

To sum up, attempts to rejuvenate Maupassant's works by adapting them for media that appeal to mass audiences confirm his enduring cultural significance and universality, while themselves being circumscribed by the production conditions and technical demands of the medium chosen. Whereas pedestrian imitation merely sends one back to the original texts to confirm their superiority, the most satisfactory and original adaptations tend to be those that adopt an initial scenario, idea or attitude from the source author and use it in an entirely new setting (so that the presence of the original author is barely visible). As a result, however, demonstrating influence becomes problematic or simply irrelevant. Thus French critics like to claim John Ford's classic western *Stagecoach* (1939) as a brilliant imitation of 'Boule de suif', whereas Ford's biographer points out that Dudley Nichols's screenplay actually derives from an Ernest Haycox story, 'Stage to

Lordsburg'.[19] Referencing an iconic classic author as the source of a film or other adaptation is more often a marketing ploy to launch the new product than a meaningful aesthetic statement about the relationship between the original and a copy.

Might the same be said about Maupassant's influence on literary authors and particularly storywriters? Insofar as Maupassant established a paradigm for the skilfully plotted and crafted story that dextrously evokes tragicomic dilemmas in a realistic setting, his potential heirs include a legion of later writers (many of them writing outside France in other languages) who have preferred traditional narration, readability and clarity to the formal innovations and indeterminacy of modernism (whose major exponents in fiction include Proust, Joyce and Kafka).[20] While tracing specific intertextual links between writers is always problematic, in some cases at least the creative debt of more traditional realists to Maupassant is evident, if not always acknowledged. Three striking examples of popular literary storytellers whose accessibility and imaginative craftsmanship are analogous to Maupassant's and won them large audiences in the early and mid-twentieth century are provided by O. Henry in the USA, Marcel Aymé in France and Somerset Maugham in the UK.[21] As a novelist, Maupassant is a more oblique reference point (because his best novels are themselves modelled on Balzac, Flaubert and Zola). But if *Bel-Ami* is taken as a model in its account of ruthless *arrivisme*, its distant heirs include novels like Tom Wolfe's *Bonfire of the Vanities* (1987) and Aravind Adiga's *The White Tiger* (winner of the Man Booker Prize in 2008), which updates and transfers Maupassant's bleak account of *fin-de-siècle* France to contemporary India.[22] What is certainly clear is not only that Maupassant's work continues to be read or seen by millions of readers and viewers, but that his concept of fiction-writing and Darwinian view of human society have shaped the narrative techniques and collective imagination of innumerable prose writers.

In other words, Maupassant's writing successfully fulfils and sustains certain expectations about literary fiction and its relationship with readers and society more broadly. It must entice and engage readers affectively and imaginatively (by absorbing them into an intelligible and plausible story and fictional world), but also obey certain moral and aesthetic imperatives. These include offering an objective and comprehensive account of human suffering and social abuses, while communicating the sensual intensity of human experience and desire in language that is both precise and illuminating. If Maupassant is anxious to distance himself from mere entertainers (who beguile undemanding readers with gripping stories that recycle the commonplaces and stereotypes of popular fiction), it is because he has much greater ambitions, in terms of psychological insight, verisimilitude and literary artistry. As regards his supposed imitators, this is patently not the case with an immensely popular writer like O. Henry, whose much anthologized stories (such as 'The Gift of the Magi', 1906) are mainly memorable for ingenious plot reversals sustained with a mixture of humour and sentimentality, all of which may strike twenty-first-century readers as somewhat contrived and dated. On the other hand, Maupassant's laconic clarity and sharpness of style and vision also distinguish him from the oblique and opaque manner often favoured by more demanding literary storytellers around the turn of the twentieth century, like Villiers de l'Isle Adam, Henry James, Chekhov and Conrad. Although Maupassant actually shares the subject matter and social attitudes of these celebrated writers (such as a fondness for the exotic and macabre, a fascination with the strife and cruelty underpinning social relations, a preference for ironic detachment and dislike of didacticism), the experience of reading his stories as opposed to theirs is often strikingly different. Whereas Maupassant's naturalistic style, sharply delineated characters and setting, and insistence on spatial and temporal coherence (even between and within embedded narratives) allow the reader to be effortlessly absorbed into his tales, Villiers, James, Chekhov and Conrad all disrupt such traditional storytelling conventions. Thus while Maupassant's 'Le Horla' and James's *The Turn of the Screw* (1898) are both compelling stories about ghostly possession which leave the ultimate cause a mystery, readers of James's much longer novella are likely to be equally mystified by the intricacies and obscurities of the storytelling process itself. Even at the level of syntax, Villiers, James and Conrad sometimes verge on the unintelligible, confounding the reader's urge to decipher their narratives (and making titles like *Contes cruels*, *The Turn of the Screw* and *Heart of Darkness* seem singularly appropriate).

Maupassant's successors in the twentieth century were literary storytellers who eschewed formal experimentation and avant-garde posturing; predictably, they were favoured by ordinary readers, and despised or ignored by highbrow critics and writers, who regarded the innovations of symbolism, surrealism or the *nouveau roman* as more culturally significant. These popular storytellers' aesthetic conservatism and commercial success were often associated with political conservatism: one thinks, for example, of Rudyard Kipling and Somerset Maugham (whose sympathetic accounts of the British Empire arouse suspicion even today), or Marcel Aymé (who made the unfortunate decision to publish stories in collaborationist journals during the German occupation of France in the 1940s and was virulently anti-Gaullist and anti-communist). All three were brilliantly inventive storytellers who, like Maupassant, delight and engage readers by their ability to evoke both familiar and exotic places, characters, and dramatic confrontations between classes and cultures, in a few telling details, with understated humour and pathos. While all three emulated Maupassant by producing stories that skilfully turn banal mishaps and encounters into micro-tragedies of social reportage and satirical observation, they considerably extended Maupassant's range. Kipling was also an immensely popular poet, and both Maugham and Aymé had lucrative careers as dramatists. As storytellers, both Kipling and Aymé were particularly successful in their charmingly inventive fables ostensibly written for children (for example in *The Jungle Book* series of 1894–5 and *Les Contes du chat perché* in 1934).[23]

The Francophile Maugham (who was born and died in France) openly admitted that his early novels and stories were indebted to Maupassant, Zola and Huysmans, whose naturalistic frankness about sexuality, poverty and corruption were still perceived as indecently scandalous in Edwardian England.[24] Unlike his contemporary André Gide, Maugham never publicly avowed or wrote about his homosexuality, although his fondness for displaying naked male flesh and cynical depiction of marital relations in his stories tacitly reveal his preferences. His insistent depiction of frustrated love and desire, of the struggle for power in personal and social relations, of the naive hypocrisies of polite society, all reveal an affinity with Maupassant which is reaffirmed in memorable stories that sometimes read like inspired pastiches of his French master. Maugham travels beyond Maupassant's exotic Mediterranean locales to encompass more distant outposts of empire (whether British or American), in the Far East or South Seas.

One of his most celebrated novellas, 'Rain' (1921), effectively reprises 'Boule de suif' in its initial plot configuration, although the outcome is notably different. When a disparate group of people crossing the Pacific by ship are stranded for weeks in western Samoa during a measles epidemic, they discover that one traveller is a prostitute called Sadie Thompson. She enterprisingly resumes her trade, only to be thwarted by a Protestant missionary, who persuades the authorities to have her deported to San Francisco, where she faces a prison sentence. Sadie's defiant resistance is broken and she humiliatingly submits to all the inflexible missionary's demands (which include not merely renouncing sin but enduring a prison sentence as penance). But after several intimate encounters with his humbled convert, the missionary suddenly commits suicide. Sadie denounces his bestial behaviour and returns to prostitution, having apparently outwitted her adversary. Although 'Rain' appears to reverse the conclusion of 'Boule de suif' (with the puritanical missionary presumably succumbing to sexual temptation and destroyed by his own sinfulness), Maugham, like Maupassant, adroitly refrains from drawing explicit psychological or moral judgements from this clash of personalities and beliefs. Both antagonists are presented with studied ambiguity. Thus for all his stiff-necked self-righteousness, the missionary is sincere in his beliefs and altruistic in intent, whereas Sadie is easy-going but coarsely devoid of scruples. We are left uncertain whether he actually acted as a sexual aggressor (as she implies) or was manipulated and duped by her perhaps faked conversion.

A recent biographer of Maugham observes that he captures 'not the big picture . . . but the small lives of unremarkable individuals struggling to create the reassuringly ordinary out of an extravagantly exotic environment'. He was 'beloved by unliterary, unofficial, unacademic humanity', earning vast sums for film rights and selling almost 80 million copies of his books worldwide in a career that lasted over half a century. Yet when friends tried to publish a celebratory Festschrift after his death in 1965, most of the literati and critics they approached declined to contribute.[25] While Maugham benefited in his own lifetime from the popularization and democratization of culture that Maupassant enjoyed only posthumously, he has not achieved the latter's rehabilitation as an author who still provides both simple and sophisticated pleasures to all types of readers and is an indispensable reference point in the evolution of short fiction.

References

1 A Life

1   For example, M. G. Lerner, *Maupassant* (London, 1975); Francis
    Steegmuller, *Maupassant* (London, 1950); Edward D. Sullivan,
    Maupassant the Novelist (Westport, CT, 1978); Marlo Johnston, *Guy
    de Maupassant* (Paris, 2012); Armand Lanoux, *Maupassant le Bel-Ami*
    (Paris, 1979); Paul Morand, *Vie de Guy de Maupassant* [1942] (Paris,
    1998); Nadine Satiat, *Maupassant* (Paris, 2003); François Tassart,
    Souvenirs sur Guy de Maupassant (Paris, 1911); André Vial, *Guy de
    Maupassant et l'art du roman* (Paris, 1971); Maria Giulia Longhi,
    Introduzione a Maupassant (Rome, 1994).
2   A useful recent compilation is *Guy de Maupassant's Selected Works*,
    ed. Robert Lethbridge (New York and London, 2017), which includes
    thirty stories (10 per cent of his output).
3   Georges Normandy, *La Fin de Maupassant* (Paris, 1927), p. 17.
4   Guy de Maupassant, *Oeuvres complètes* (unpaginated Arvensa Kindle
    edition).
5   Multiplying by twelve gives a very rough idea in 2020 pounds sterling
    of the equivalent of 1880s prices in francs.
6   *Oeuvres complètes.*
7   Maupassant, *Chroniques* (Paris, 1980), vol. III, p. 169.
8   For details, see Roger Price, *A Social History of Nineteenth-century France*
    (London, 1987).
9   *Oeuvres complètes.*
10 Francis Steegmuller, ed., *The Letters of Gustave Flaubert, 1857–1880*
    (London, 1982), p. 243.
11 Maupassant, *Contes et nouvelles*, ed. Louis Forestier (Paris, 1974), vol. I,
    p. 1110.
12 Johnston, *Guy de Maupassant.*

13 Edmond and Jules de Goncourt, *Journal* (Paris, 1989), vol. ii, pp. 741–2. Goncourt also recalled anecdotes about Maupassant's sexual exhibitionism in brothels on 9 April 1893, vol. iii, p. 811.

14 *Oeuvres complètes*.

15 Ibid.

16 See Roy Porter, *The Greatest Benefit to Mankind: A Medical History of Humanity from Antiquity to the Present* (London, 1997); Roger L. Williams, *The Horror of Life* (London, 1980).

17 Jacques-Louis Douchin, *La Vie érotique de Guy de Maupassant* (Paris, 1986), p. 136.

18 Lerner, *Maupassant*, p. 211.

19 *Oeuvres complètes*.

20 Ibid.

21 Ibid.

22 Cited by Johnston, p. 611.

23 For example by Forestier in his notes to *Contes et nouvelles*, vol. i, p. 1424.

24 For a detailed socio-economic analysis of late nineteenth-century literary production, see Pierre Bourdieu, *Les Règles de l'art: genèse et structure du champ littéraire* (Paris, 1992); Christophe Charle, *La Crise littéraire à l'époque du naturalisme* (Paris, 1979).

25 Maupassant's even more successful contemporary Émile Zola shared his opinion that the possibility of earning large sums emancipated writers from the whims of patronage, and that 'tout producteur doit être l'artisan de sa fortune'. But he adds that in practice, most novelists earned only 2,000 francs for a book and many journalists earned no more than 3,000 francs annually. See 'L'Argent dans la littérature' (1880), in *Le Roman expérimental* (Paris, 1971), pp. 193–6.

26 For example, Forestier, *Contes et nouvelles*, vol. ii, p. 1523.

27 *Chroniques*, vol. iii, p. 130.

28 *Oeuvres complètes*.

29 *Oeuvres complètes*.

30 Robert Lethbridge unfortunately mistranslates this as 'fawn', making the writer an unlikely predecessor of Bambi: *Maupassant's Selected Works*, p. 275.

31 *Oeuvres complètes*.

32 See Lethbridge, *Maupassant's Selected Works*, for further samples.

33 Morand, *Vie de Guy de Maupassant*, p. 68.

34 See the encyclopaedia *Quid 2007* (Paris, 2006), p. 555b.

35 See www.lefigaro.fr (accessed May 2017).

2 Journalist

1 Maupassant, *Oeuvres complètes* (unpaginated Arvensa Kindle edition).

2 Maupassant, *Chroniques*, ed. Hubert Juin (Paris, 1980), vol. III,
   pp. 165–6.

3 See *Études, chroniques et correspondance,* ed. René Dumesnil (Paris,
   1938); *Maupassant journaliste et chroniqueur,* ed. Gérard Delaisement
   (Paris, 1956); *Chroniques,* ed. Gérard Delaisement (Paris, 2003);
   Chroniques, ed. Henri Mitterand (Paris, 2008); *Selected Works,* ed.
   Robert Lethbridge (New York and London, 2017).

4 Christophe Charle, *Le Siècle de la presse* (Paris, 2004), p. 201. Much of
   the information in the preceding paragraphs is synthesized from this
   source.

5 Ibid., p. 218.

6 Thomas Ferenczi, *L'Invention du journalisme en France: naissance de la
   presse moderne à la fin du XIXe siècle* (Paris, 1993).

7 *Bel-Ami*, ed. Marie-Claire Bancquart (Paris, 1979), p. 11.

8 Ferenczi, *L'Invention du journalisme en France*, p. 63.

9 Claude Bellanger et al., eds, *Histoire générale de la presse française*
   (Paris, 1972), vol. III, p. 380; André Lajeune-Vilar, *Les Coulisses de la
   presse: moeurs et chantage du journalisme* (Paris, 1895), p. 260.

10 See for example readers' reviews of Henri Mitterand's edition of the
    Chroniques at amazon.fr, accessed January 2018.

11 Jules Lemaître, *Les Contemporains* (Paris, 1887), vol. III, pp. 261–6.

12 *Chroniques*, vol. III, pp. 41–2.

13 *Chroniques*, vol. I, p. 5.

14   Ibid., p. 291.

15 *Chroniques*, vol. III, pp. 28–9.

16 *Chroniques*, vol. I, p. 140.

17 Ibid., p. 149.

18 The story 'Enragée?' (1883) does in fact make fun of an innocent bride
    who mistakes sexual arousal for incipient rabies.

19 See Roy Porter, *The Greatest Benefit to Mankind: A Medical History of Humanity from Antiquity to the Present* (London, 1997), p. 435.

20 *Chroniques*, vol. II, p. 216.

21 *Chroniques*, vol. I, p. 102.

22 Ibid., pp. 7–8.

23 *Chroniques*, vol. II, p. 228.

24 *Chroniques*, vol. III, p. 385.

25 *Chroniques*, vol. I, p. 323.

26 Ibid., p. 106.

27 *Chroniques*, vol. II, p. 16.

28 *Chroniques*, vol. I, pp. 365–6.

29 *Chroniques*, vol. II, pp. 65–6.

30 Ibid., p. 274.

31 Ibid., p. 94.

32 See Roger Price, *A Social History of Nineteenth-century France* (London, 1987). A single mining disaster in 1906 killed 1,200 men, for example.

33 See for example L. Gaudefroy-Demombynes, *La Femme dans l'oeuvre de Maupassant* (Paris, 1943).

34 Chantal Jennings, 'La Dualité de Maupassant: son attitude envers la femme', *Revue des sciences humaines*, 140 (1970), pp. 559–78.

35 *Chroniques*, vol. I, p. 65.

36 *Études, chroniques et correspondance*, p. 101.

37 *Chroniques*, vol. II, p. 281.

38 *Chroniques*, vol. I, pp. 127–30.

39 Ibid., pp. 99 and 114.

40 *Chroniques*, vol. II, pp. 87–8.

41 *Chroniques*, vol. III, pp. 210–11.

42 *Chroniques*, vol. II, p. 33.

43 Ibid., p. 82.

44 *Chroniques*, vol. I, p. 334.

45 Ibid., pp. 230 and 400.

46 Maupassant, *Contes et nouvelles* (Paris, 1974), vol. II, p. 754.

47 *Chroniques*, vol. II, pp. 190–91.

48 Ibid., p. 55.

49 Ibid., p. 430.

50 *Bel-Ami*, ed. Gérard Delaisement (Paris, 1959), p. lxxvii.

3 Writer

1 Jules Lemaitre, *Les Contemporains* (Paris, 1899), vol. v, p. 9.

2 Maupassant, *Chroniques*, ed. Henri Mitterand (Paris, 2008).

3 See for example the critical editions of Maupassant's stories and novels published in Gallimard's Pléiade series, edited by Louis Forestier (Paris, 1974, 1979, 1987). Some examples will be discussed in later chapters. All subsequent references are to these editions.

4 See Yvan Leclerc, 'Maupassant théoricien', in *Maupassant aujourd'hui*, ed. Laure Helms and Jean Louis-Cabanès (Paris, 2008), pp. 17–33.

5 Cited in Marlo Johnston, *Guy de Maupassant* (Paris, 2012), pp. 521, 794 and 863.

6 All quotations from Maupassant's correspondence are from his *Oeuvres complètes* (unpaginated Arvensa Kindle edition).

7 Maupassant, *Chroniques*, ed. Hubert Juin (Paris, 1980), vol. ii, p. 328.

8 *Chroniques*, vol. iii, p. 241.

9 *Chroniques*, vol. i, p. 20.

10 Ibid., p. 19.

11 Ibid., p. 65.

12 Ibid., p. 285.

13 *Chroniques*, vol. ii, p. 13.

14 Ibid., p. 21.

15 Ibid., pp. 197 and 199.

16 Maupassant, *Romans*, ed. Louis Forestier (Paris, 1987), p. 713.

17 *Chroniques*, vol. ii, p. 41.

18 Ibid., p. 130.

19 *Chroniques*, vol. iii, pp. 83, 85, 111 and 110.

20 *Romans*, pp. 706–15.

21 Cited in Johnston, *Guy de Maupassant*, p. 308.

22 All quotations from Maupassant's travel writing, poetry and plays are from his *Oeuvres complètes* (unpaginated Arvensa Kindle edition).

23 Cited by Johnston, *Guy de Maupassant*, p. 178.

24 Louis Forestier, '"La Meilleure Garce": Observations sur *Des vers* de Maupassant', *Dix-neuf/Vingt*, 6 (1998), pp. 25–41, 29 and 34.

25 All of Maupassant's known poetry has now been published in *Oeuvres poétiques complètes*, ed. Emmanuel Vincent (Rouen, 2001).

26 Marie-Claire Bancquart, ed., *La Parure et autres contes parisiens* (Paris, 1984), p. 66.

27 Floriane Place-Verghnes, 'Maupassant pornographe', *Neophilologus*, 85 (2001), pp. 501–17.

28 Maupassant, *Contes et nouvelles*, ed. Louis Forestier (Paris, 1974 and 1979), vol. i, p. 488.

29 See Claudine Giachetti, 'De la filiation et de l'adoption : Maupassant et le code civil', in *Maupassant aujourd'hui*, pp. 183–96.

30 See Richard Fusco, *Maupassant and the American Short Story* (University Park, pa, 1994).

31 Edmond and Jules de Goncourt, *Journal: mémoires de la vie littéraire* (Paris, 1989), vol. iii, p. 87.

32 See Bernard Demont, 'Quelques dimensions du paysage dans les contes et nouvelles de Maupassant', in *Maupassant aujourd'hui*, pp. 161–72.

33 Mitterand, ed., *Chroniques* (unpaginated Kindle edition).

34 Marcel Cressot, *La Phrase et le vocabulaire de J.-K. Huysmans* (Paris, 1938).

35 Jacques Dubois, *Romanciers français de l'instantané au xixe siècle* (Brussels, 1963).

36 André Vial, *Guy de Maupassant et l'art du roman* (Paris, 1954), pp. 577–609.

37 Émile Zola, *Le Roman expérimental* (Paris, 1971), pp. 219–20.

4 Storyteller

1 Jonathan Gottschalk, *The Storytelling Animal: How Stories Make Us Human* (Boston and New York, 2013), p. xiv.

2 Oliver Sacks, *The Man who Mistook his Wife for a Hat* (London, 1986), p. 105.

3 Yuval Noah Harari, *Sapiens: A Brief History of Humanity* (London, 2014).

4 See René Godenne, *La Nouvelle française* (Paris, 1974) and Peter Cogman, *Narration in Nineteenth-century French Short Fiction* (Durham, 2002).

5 For example, *Contes et nouvelles*, ed. Louis Forestier (Paris, 1974 and 1979).

6 See Emanuèle Grandadam, *Contes et nouvelles de Maupassant: pour une poétique du recueil* (Rouen, 2007).

7   Maupassant, *Études, chroniques et correspondance*, ed. René Dumesnil (Paris, 1938).

8   For example: *'La Parure' et autres contes parisiens*, ed. Marie-Claire Bancquart (Paris, 1984); *'Le Horla' et autres contes cruels et fantastiques*, ed. Marie-Claire Bancquart (Paris, 1976); *'Le Horla' et autres contes d'angoisse*, ed. Antonia Fonyi (Paris, 1984); *'Boule de suif' et autres contes de la guerre*, ed. W. M. Landers (London, 1982).

9   Maupassant, *Contes et nouvelles, 1884–1890* (Paris, 1988), pp. 252–4.

10 For a discussion of the alleged factual basis, see Richard Bolster, '"Boule de suif": une source documentaire?', *Revue d'histoire littéraire de la France* (November–December 1984), pp. 901–8.

11 Landers, ed., *'Boule de suif'*, p. 16.

12 M. G. Lerner, *Maupassant* (London, 1975), p. 172.

13 Robert Lethbridge, ed., *Guy de Maupassant's Selected Works* (New York and London, 2017), p. xiv.

14 André Vial, *Guy de Maupassant et l'art du roman* (Paris, 1954), p. 460.

15 E. D. Sullivan, *Maupassant: The Short Stories* (London, 1962), p. 11.

16 As Rosamund Bartlett writes, 'Discarding the traditional plot-driven structure of the short story liberated Chekhov from having to observe other conventions. It meant that he could begin and end his stories inconclusively, for example, and challenge his readers' perceptions of what made a short story.' Anton Chekhov, *About Love and Other Stories*, trans. R. Bartlett (Oxford, 2004), p. xxi.

17 Vial, *Guy de Maupassant et l'art du roman*, p. 444.

18 Richard Fusco, *Maupassant and the American Short Story* (University Park, PA, 1994).

19 Bernard Haezewindt, *Guy de Maupassant: de l'anecdote au conte littéraire* (Amsterdam and Atlanta, GA, 1993).

20 *Contes et nouvelles*, ed. Louis Forestier, vol. I, pp. 58–9.

21 Ibid., p. 1288.

22 Ibid., p. 64.

23 Léon Tolstoy, *Zola, Dumas, Guy de Maupassant*, trans. E. Halpérine-Kaminsky (Paris, 1896), p. 104.

24 *Contes et nouvelles*, vol. I, p. 650.

25 Jean-Paul Sartre, *Qu'est-ce que la littérature?* (Paris, 1978), p. 174.

26 *Contes et nouvelles*, vol. I, p. 1296.

27 Ibid., pp. 89–90.

28 Ibid., pp. 97 and 111.

29 Ibid., p. 119.

30 Ibid., p. 1308.

31 Ibid., p. 101.

32 Francis Steegmuller, *Maupassant* (London, 1950), pp. 193 and 197.

33 *Contes et nouvelles*, vol. I, p. 765.

34 Haezewindt, *Guy de Maupassant: de l'anecdote au conte littéraire*, p. 191.

35 Lethbridge, *Guy de Maupassant's Selected Works*, p. xviii.

36 Haezewindt, *Guy de Maupassant: de l'anecdote au conte littéraire*, p. 191.

37 *Contes et nouvelles*, vol. I, p. 1198.

38 Haezewindt, *Guy de Maupassant: de l'anecdote au conte littéraire*, p. 191.

39 *Contes et nouvelles*, vol. I, p. 1204.

40 Ibid., p. 1205.

41 See Micheline Besnard-Coursodon, *Étude thématique et structurale de l'oeuvre de Maupassant: le piège* (Paris, 1973).

42 See Sigmund Freud, 'A Seventeenth-century Demonological Neurosis', in *The Ego and the Id and Other Works* (London, 1961), p. 72. Both Freud and Maupassant attended the famous alienist Charcot's Paris lectures on hysterical and nervous illnesses in 1885.

43 *Contes et nouvelles*, vol. II, p. 874.

44 Ibid., p. 199.

45 Ibid., p. 311.

46 Bancquart, ed., *'Le Horla'*.

47 Tzvetan Todorov, *Introduction à la littérature fantastique* (Paris, 1970).

48 See Louis Forestier in *Contes et nouvelles*, vol. II, p. 1619.

49 Ibid., p. 913.

50 Ibid., p. 921.

51 Fusco, *Maupassant and the American Short Story*, pp. 58 and 48.

52 Todorov, *Introduction à la littérature fantastique*, p. 111.

53 *Contes et nouvelles*, vol. II, p. 1182.

54 Ibid., p. 1204.

55 Ibid., pp. 1190 and 1203.

56 Maupassant, *Chroniques* (Paris, 1980), vol. I, p. 104.

5 Novelist

1 J. A. Cuddon, *A Dictionary of Literary Terms* (Harmondsworth, 1979), p. 432.
2 Maupassant, *Chroniques* (Paris, 1980), vol. III, p. 378.
3 Ibid., pp. 379–84.
4 See Claudine Giacchetti, *Maupassant: espaces du roman* (Geneva, 1993).
5 Maupassant, *Romans*, ed. Louis Forestier (Paris, 1987), p. 1436.
6 Ibid., p. 1495.
7 Ibid., pp. 709–10.
8 Ibid., p. xxxii.
9 In an 1881 letter to Gisèle d'Estoc, in *Oeuvres complètes* (unpaginated Arvensa Kindle edition).
10 Paul Ignotus, *The Paradox of Maupassant* (London, 1966), p. 223.
11 *Romans*, p. xxvii.
12 Ibid., p. 1236.
13 Ibid., pp. 5 and 26.
14 Ibid., p. 66.
15 Ibid., p. 110.
16 Ibid., p. 115.
17 Ibid., pp. xxvii and 1239.
18 Ibid., p. 194.
19 La Rochefoucauld, *Maximes* (Paris, 1966), p. 59.
20 *Romans*, p. 7.
21 'Aux critiques de *Bel-Ami*', in *Romans*, pp. 1343–6.
22 Ibid., pp. 249–50.
23 Ibid., p. 307.
24 Ibid., p. 478.
25 Ibid., p. 467.
26 Ibid., p. 478.
27 Ibid., p. 472.
28 *Bel-Ami*, trans. Douglas Parmée (London, 1975), p. 20.
29 *Bel-Ami*, ed. Gérard Delaisement (Paris, 1959), p. xi.
30 *Romans*, p. 214.
31 Roy Porter, *The Greatest Benefit to Mankind: A Medical History of Humanity from Antiquity to the Present* (London, 1997), pp. 267 and 392.
32 *Romans*, p. 523.

33 Ibid., p. 631.

34 Ibid., p. 1422.

35 Ibid., pp. 500 and 543.

36 Ibid., p. 560.

37 Ibid., p. 656.

38 Ibid., pp. 612–13.

39 Ibid., p. 674.

40 Ibid., p. 698.

41 See Edward D. Sullivan, *Maupassant the Novelist* (Westport, CT, 1978), p. 106.

42 Robert Lethbridge, *Maupassant: Pierre et Jean* (London, 1984), p. 44.

43 *Romans*, p. 798.

44 Ibid., p. 726.

45 Ibid., p. 749.

46 Ibid., p. 809.

47 Ibid., p. 817.

48 Ibid., p. 822.

49 Ibid., p. 823.

50 Ibid., p. 722.

51 Ibid., p. 832.

52 Ibid., p. 761. Sartre's 'evocations of the viscous, the fluid, the paste-like' nature of reality in *La Nausée* (Nausea) are meant to challenge the relationship between self and phenomena in a more fundamental, ontological sense, rather than merely portray a disenchanted individual as Maupassant does. See Iris Murdoch, *Sartre* (London, 1967), p. 19.

53 *Romans*, p. 1560.

54 Francis Steegmuller, *Maupassant* (London, 1950), p. 271.

55 'Bourget enjoyed writing about the piously conservative, but above all he preferred his characters to be fashionable and wealthy; and when he described the latter he adopted their own tone. His novels are filled with a parvenu obsession with the trivia of high-life, with a reverence for the more fashionable outer manifestations of Catholicism, with a stereo-typed anti-Semitism (Bourget was opposed to any attempt to right the injustice done Dreyfus), with a lip-service to something called "Art", all of which suffocate [one] as one reads.' Ibid., p. 267.

56 Sullivan, *Maupassant the Novelist*, pp. 141 and 147.

57 André Vial, *Guy de Maupassant et l'art du roman* (Paris, 1954), pp. 374 and 10. For a balanced discussion, see Trevor A. Le V. Harris, *Maupassant et Fort comme la mort: le roman contrefait* (Paris, 1991).

58 *Romans*, p. 1012.

59 Ibid., p. 1571.

60 Ibid., p. 1028.

61 Ibid., pp. 875–7.

62 Ibid., p. 986.

63 Ibid., p. 1033.

64 See Mary Donaldson-Evans, *A Woman's Revenge: The Chronology of Dispossession in Maupassant's Fiction* (Lexington, KY, 1986).

65 See Emmanuel Vincent, 'Genèse des derniers romans', in *Maupassant aujourd'hui*, ed. Laure Helms and Jean-Louis Cabanès (Paris, 2008), pp. 87–111.

6 Ironist

1 See Maupassant, *Contes et nouvelles*, ed. Louis Forestier (Paris, 1974 and 1979), vol. I, p. 1613.

2 Pierre Cogny, *Maupassant l'homme sans Dieu* (Paris, 1968), pp. 30 and 39.

3 Mariane Bury, 'Le Goût de Maupassant pour l'équivoque', *Dix-neuf/Vingt*, 6 (1998), pp. 83–94, 85 and 87.

4 For a more detailed discussion, see J. A. Cuddon, *A Dictionary of Literary Terms* (Harmondsworth, 1982), pp. 335–40.

5 For a discussion of the literary background, see Christopher Robinson, *French Literature in the Nineteenth Century* (London, 1978).

6 Maupassant, *Chroniques* (Paris, 1980), vol. II, pp. 111–12.

7 *Contes et nouvelles*, vol. I, p. 728.

8 The story 'A cheval' also replicates an incident that occurred to Schopenhauer, who was condemned to pay compensation to an elderly woman whom he accidentally knocked down; this may be purely coincidental.

9 Arthur Schopenhauer, *Essays and Aphorisms*, trans. R. J. Hollingdale (Harmondsworth, 1970), pp. 165 and 210.

10 Ibid., p. 137.

11 Ibid., p. 187.

12 Ibid., p. 41.

13 Ibid., p. 49.

14 Ibid., pp. 64 and 57.

15 Ibid., p. 155.

16 See R.-P. Colin, *Schopenhauer en France: un mythe naturaliste* (Lyon, 1979); Robert Zimmer, *Le Grand Livre des philosophes*, trans. Olivier Mannoni (Paris, 2016).

17 Marie-Claire Bancquart, *Images littéraires du Paris 'fin-de-siècle'* (Paris, 1979), p. 144.

18 Herbert Spencer, *Structure, Function and Evolution*, ed. Stanislav Andreski (London, 1972), p. 26. See also Linda L. Clark, *Social Darwinism in France* (Birmingham, AL, 1984) and Laurence A. Gregorio, *Maupassant's Fiction and the Darwinian View of Life* (New York, 2005).

19 Maupassant, *Correspondance*, in *Oeuvres complètes* (unpaginated Arvensa Kindle edition).

20 See *Contes et nouvelles*, vol. II, p. 1709.

21 Ibid., p. 1208.

22 Schopenhauer, *Essays and Aphorisms*, p. 85.

23 *Contes et nouvelles*, vol. II, p. 1215.

24 Ibid., p. 1216.

25 Ibid., p. 1223.

26 *Chroniques*, vol. II, p. 158.

27 See Zimmer, *Le Grand Livre des philosophes*, for a helpful outline.

28 *Contes et nouvelles*, vol. I, pp. 1363 and 1369.

29 Maupassant, *Boule de suif and Other Stories*, trans. H.N.P. Sloman (Harmondsworth, 1946).

30 For example, J.-K. Huysmans, *Marthe: histoire d'une fille* (Brussels, 1876); Edmond de Goncourt, *La Fille Élisa* (Paris, 1877) and Émile Zola, *Nana* (Paris, 1880).

31 *Contes et nouvelles*, vol. I, p. 256.

32 *Boule de suif*, p. 208.

33 *Contes et nouvelles*, vol. I, pp. 257–8.

34 Ibid., pp. 273–5.

35 Ibid., p. 283; *Boule de suif*, p. 240.

36 Ibid., vol. I, p. 878.

37 Ibid., p. 894.

38 Ibid., p. 1450.

39 Jean-Paul Sartre, *Qu'est-ce que la littérature?* (Paris, 1978), pp. 79 and 82.

40 Mariane Bury, *La Poétique de Maupassant* (Paris, 1994), p. 53.

41 *Contes et nouvelles*, vol. I, p. 253.

7 Afterlives

1 See Artine Artinian, *Maupassant Criticism in France* (New York, 1941), and *Pour et contre Maupassant* (Paris, 1955). The responses can also be found at maupassantia.fr, accessed February 2019.

2 Information collated from his *Correspondance*, in *Oeuvres complètes* (unpaginated Kindle Arvensa edition).

3 See Marlo Johnston, *Guy de Maupassant* (Paris, 2012); Géraldi Leroy and Julie-Bertrand-Sabiani, *La Vie littéraire à la Belle Époque* (Paris, 1998); Émile Zola, 'L'Argent dans la littérature', in *Le Roman expérimental* (Paris, 1971).

4 Their works are however readily available in French digitized editions. Bourget is still considered a significant intellectual figure.

5 See Jacques Lecarme and Bruno Vercier, eds, *Maupassant miroir de la nouvelle* (Paris, 1988).

6 Such as *La Grande anthologie du fantastique*, a multi-volume collection edited by Jacques Goimard and Roland Stragliati (Paris, 1996).

7 Such as Arnold Kellett's abridged edition of *Contes du surnaturel* (London, 1969). For a critical review, see Peter Whyte in *French Studies*, XXXVI/1 (1972), p. 90.

8 See Richard Fusco, *Maupassant and the American Short Story* (University Park, PA, 1994); Johnston, *Maupassant*; Francis Steegmuller, *Maupassant* (London, 1950).

9 See David Coward, 'Traduire Maupassant', in *Maupassant conteur et romancier*, ed. Christopher Lloyd and Robert Lethbridge (Durham, 1994), pp. 1–11. Coward is himself an accomplished translator.

10 For a well-informed discussion, see Deborah Cartmell and Imelda Whelehan, eds, *Adaptations* (London, 1999).

11 *The Inn* production is available on YouTube, accessed September 2018.

12 For example, by Henri Mitterand in his edition of Maupassant's *Chroniques* (Paris, 2008).

13 See Francis Vanoye, 'Éloge de l'anachronisme: à propos de quelques adaptations cinématographiques de Maupassant', in *Maupassant aujourd'hui*, ed. Laure Helms and Jean-Louis Cabanès (Paris, 2008), pp. 333–9, and the useful filmography in the Bouquins edition of *Contes et nouvelles*, ed. Dominique Frémy et al. (Paris, 1988).

14 Luis Buñuel, *My Last Breath*, trans. Abigail Israel (London, 1985), p. 200.

15 Dard's script was published in *Paris-Théâtre*, 82 (1954), pp. 21–55.

16 See François Bernadin, 'Le Scandale de *Bel-Ami*', *La Nouvelle Critique*, 7 (1955), pp. 126–38.

17 Stephen Holden, 'A Parisian Journalist's Ruthless Liaisons', *New York Times*, 7 June 2012; Michael O'Sullivan, *Washington Post*, 8 June 2012.

18 See George Perry and Alan Aldridge, *The Penguin Book of Comics* (Harmondsworth, 1971).

19 See Vanoye, 'Éloge de l'anachronisme'; and Joseph McBride, *Searching for John Ford* (London, 2004).

20 Johnnie Gratton asserts that 'the history of short fiction during the twentieth century, at least throughout the modernist period, has in itself been one of progressive erosion of faith in the capacity of *mise en intrigue*, fictional plotting, storytelling, to reflect what is understood to be most important, most relevant, most real, and most under threat, in modern experience.' He ignores the fact that this argument only applies to a relatively small group of avant-garde writers and takes no account of the much larger mass market for more accessible fiction, often in popular genres like thrillers, romance and science fiction. See 'From the *Nouvelle* to the *Nouvellistique*', in *Short French Fiction*, ed. J. E. Flower (Exeter, 1998), pp. 122–52 (p. 148).

21 For a more detailed discussion, see Florence Goyet, *The Classic Short Story* (Cambridge, 2014) and Paul March-Russell, *The Short Story* (Edinburgh, 2009).

22 In an interview with *The Guardian* on 25 August 2017, Adiga describes Zola and Maupassant as influential 'childhood heroes', accessed at www.theguardian.com.

23 For a more detailed discussion, see Christopher Lloyd, 'Marcel Aymé: "La Carte"', in *Short French Fiction*, ed. Flower, pp. 29–41.

24 See Selina Hastings, *The Secret Lives of Somerset Maugham* (London, 2009).

25 Ibid., pp. 296, 401 and 518.

Select Bibliography

Works in French

There are innumerable editions of Maupassant's works available in the original French. For the sake of consistency, I have translated the quotations into English cited in this book from the following editions:

Chroniques, ed. Hubert Juin, 3 vols (Paris, 1980)
Contes et nouvelles, ed. Louis Forestier, 2 vols (Paris, 1974 and 1979)
Oeuvres complètes (unpaginated Arvensa Kindle edition)
Romans, ed. Louis Forestier (Paris, 1987)

Translations into English

An illustrated edition of *The Complete Works of Guy de Maupassant* has been published on Kindle by Delphi. This contains all six novels, the travelogues, most of the stories and some plays and poems. It does not include the journalism and correspondence. The many older translations are not always reliable, but the following can be recommended:

Guy de Maupassant's Selected Works, trans. Sandra Smith, ed. Robert
      Lethbridge (New York and London, 2017)
Bel-Ami, trans. Douglas Parmée (Harmondsworth, 1975)
Bel-Ami, trans. Margaret Mauldon, ed. Robert Lethbridge (Oxford, 2001)
Boule de suif and Other Stories, trans. H.N.P. Sloman (Harmondsworth,
      1946)
A Day in the Country and Other Stories, trans. David Coward (Oxford, 1990)
A Woman's Life, trans. H.N.P. Sloman (Harmondsworth, 1965)

Biographies

Douchin, Jacques-Louis, *La Vie érotique de Guy de Maupassant* (Paris, 1986)

Johnston, Marlo, *Guy de Maupassant* (Paris, 2012)

Lanoux, Armand, *Maupassant le Bel-Ami* (Paris, 1979)

Lerner, M. G., *Maupassant* (London, 1975)

Morand, Paul, *Vie de Guy de Maupassant* (Paris, 1942, reissued 1998)

Satiat, Nadine, *Maupassant* (Paris, 2003)

Steegmuller, Francis, *Maupassant* (London, 1950)

Tassart, François, *Souvenirs sur Guy de Maupassant* (Paris, 1911); available online at maupassant.free.fr

Critical and Historical Studies

Bury, Mariane, *La Poétique de Maupassant* (Paris, 1994)

Charle, Christophe, *Le Siècle de la presse (1830–1939)* (Paris, 2004)

Cogman, Peter, *Narration in Nineteenth-century French Short Fiction* (Durham, 2002)

Donaldson-Evans, Mary, *A Woman's Revenge: The Chronology of Dispossession in Maupassant's Fiction* (Lexington, KY, 1986)

Ferenczi, Thomas, *L'Invention du journalisme en France: naissance de la presse moderne à la fin du XIXe siècle* (Paris, 1993)

Forestier, Louis, ed., *Maupassant et l'écriture* (Paris, 1993)

Fusco, Richard, *Maupassant and the American Short Story* (University Park, PA, 1994)

Godenne, René, *La Nouvelle française* (Paris, 1974)

Goyet, Florence, *The Classic Short Story, 1870–1925* (Cambridge, 2014)

Haezewindt, Bernard, *Guy de Maupassant: de l'anecdote au conte littéraire* (Amsterdam and Atlanta, GA, 1993)

Helms, Laure, and Jean-Louis Cabanès, eds, *Maupassant aujourd'hui* (Paris, 2008)

Lethbridge, Robert, *Maupassant: Pierre et Jean* (London, 1984)

Lloyd, Christopher, *Maupassant: Bel-Ami* (London, 1988)

Lloyd, Christopher, and Robert Lethbridge, eds, *Maupassant conteur et romancier* (Durham, 1994)

Price, Roger, *A Social History of Nineteenth-century France* (London, 1987)

Sullivan, E. D., *Maupassant: The Short Stories* (London, 1962)

—, *Maupassant the Novelist* (Westport, CT, 1978)

Vial, André, *Guy de Maupassant et l'art du roman* (Paris, 1954)

Acknowledgements

My first book on Maupassant was published more than thirty years ago. Since then, I have accumulated many debts of gratitude to friends, students and colleagues who have offered opinions, ideas and advice. In particular, I would like to thank David Baguley, Mariane Bury, Jean-Louis Cabanès, Peter Cogman, Pierre Cogny, Mary Donaldson-Evans, Louis Forestier, Bernard Haezewindt, Marlo Johnston, Robert Lethbridge, Floriane Place-Verghnes and Peter Whyte. This book is dedicated to the memory of Lucille Cairns, Angela Kershaw and Andrea Noble, whose lives, like Maupassant's, were tragically cut short.

Photo Acknowledgements

The author and publishers wish to express their thanks to the below sources of illustrative material and/or permission to reproduce it.

Photo Agoston.hu: p. 31; anonymous photo: p. 19; Barnes Foundation, Philadelphia, PA: p. 165; photo Bibliothèque Universitaire de Santé, Paris/Wikimedia France: pp. 36, 62; from *The Bookman*, vol. XVI (August 1902–February 1903): p. 63; from Jules Claretie, *Histoire de la Révolution de 1870–71 illustrée* (Paris, 1874): p. 100; Courtauld Institute of Art, London: p. 131; Frankfurt University Library: pp. 154, 155; photos Library of Congress, Washington, DC (Prints and Photographs Division): pp. 101, 143; from Guy de Maupassant, 'Miss Harriet', *Oeuvres complètes illustrées de Guy de Maupassant* (Paris, 1901): pp. 105, 116, 169; Musée des Augustins, Toulouse: p. 166; Musée d'Orsay, Paris: p. 31; Museu Paulista, São Paulo, Brazil (photo Museu Paulista (USP) Collection/Wikimedia Users Group of Brazil): p. 35; photos 'Nadar' [Gaspard-Félix Tournachon]: pp. 56, 60, 80; photo Eugène Renouard: p. 16; photo Shmyg: p. 12; photo Smithsonian Institution Libraries, Washington, DC: p. 156; from Marie Vaudouer, *Oeuvres choisies de madame de Girardin* (Paris, n.d.): p. 121; photo Émile Zola: p. 83.

Arturo Espinosa, the copyright holder of the image on p. 144, and Guilhem Vellut, the copyright holder of the image on p. 177, have published these online under conditions imposed by a Creative Commons Attribution 2.0 Generic license; Uwe Brodrecht, the copyright holder of the image on p. 149, has published it online under conditions imposed by a Creative Commons Attribution-Share Alike 2.0 Generic license; Schneiderant, the copyright holder of the image on p. 11, and Stanzilla, the copyright holder of the image on p. 174, have published them online under conditions